Praise for *Write That Book Already!*

"I learned more from this wise, witty primer of publishing than from fifteen years in the business. With everything you need to know—and some things you don't want to—in one place, this is the only pen-to-shelf guide you'll ever need."

—Jacquelyn Mitchard, author of *The Deep End of the Ocean*

"If I can't have the enablers to kick me in the pants every writing day, at least I've got this book!"

—Andrew Sean Greer, author of *The Story of a Marriage*

"If you read one book this year, I'd say you're not an avid reader. But if you *write* one book this year, this is the book you should read so you can get it published."

—Alan Zweibel, Thurber Prize–winning author of *The Other Shulman*

"*Write That Book Already!* is the most informative, interesting, useful, and fun book about the business, art, and craft of book writing since . . . well, since ever! Terrific writing, business, and human advice by some terrific, experienced, funny, smart writers. Kathi Goldmark and Sam Barry, as the Author Enablers, have been the Go-To People for aspiring writers for years, and in this book they elucidate pretty much every aspect of the craft. This book is a must-have for every aspiring writer on the planet."

—John Lescroart, author of *Treasure Hunt*

"Among the many charms of this guide to becoming a writer, it consistently helps you understand the perspective of the agents, editors, and gatekeepers who you probably fear are in your way, but are in fact there to help you if you're willing to listen. Anyone at work on their first book, or wanting to start their first book, should soak up some of this tough love from Kathi and Sam."

—Po Bronson, author of *What Should I Do with My Life?*

This stellar new book on writing
Is most helpful, clear, and inviting.
The big kicker, though—
I feel you must know—
Is its humor, which just keeps delighting.

—David Corbett, author of *Do They Know I'm Running?*

"It's the book you need in your back pocket and under your pillow so you never feel alone on that long, mysterious road from blank page to bestseller list."

—Jewelle Gomez, author of *The Gilda Stories*

"Too chicken to start writing that bestseller in your head? Read this book, but only if you can handle success."

—Bharati Mukherjee, author of *Jasmine* and *Desirable Daughters*

"A playful but practical guide that contains just about everything I've told my own writing students over the last thirty years."

—Molly Giles, author of *Creek Walk and Other Stories* and *Iron Shoes*

"With humor, compassion, wisdom, and street smarts, this wonderful book takes aspiring writers by the hand and guides them through the publication process, from first inspiration to bookstore shelf, with a matzo ball soup break (recipe included!) on the way. If you want to write and get published, you need this book."

—Elizabeth Dewberry, author of *His Lovely Wife*

"Kathi Goldmark and Sam Barry are the literary older siblings every new writer needs—encouraging, sensible, and funny as hell. They'll cheer you up even as they tell it straight, in a book filled with good advice, helpful hints, and great anecdotes from marquee names in the world of publishing. Read their book, already! It will Enable you—and entertain you—on the way to writing your own."

—Sylvia Brownrigg, author of *Morality Tale* and *Pages for You*

WRITE THAT
BOOK
ALREADY!

Foreword by Maya Angelou

WRITE THAT BOOK

ALREADY!

The Tough Love You Need to Get Published *Now*

Includes Original Insight from
Stephen King, Amy Tan, Dave Barry,
Scott Turow, Andrew Sean Greer, Meg
Waite Clayton...
and a whole bunch more

Sam Barry and Kathi Kamen Goldmark,
BookPage's Author Enablers

adamsmedia
Avon, Massachusetts

For Tony, Marissa, Daniel, and Laura, terrific writers all

Published by
Adams Media, a division of F+W Media, Inc.
57 Littlefield Street, Avon, MA 02322. U.S.A.
www.adamsmedia.com

ISBN 10: 1-60550-147-6
ISBN 13: 978-1-60550-147-5

eISBN 10: 1-4405-0710-4
eISBN 13: 978-1-4405-0710-6

Printed in the United States of America.

10   9   8   7   6   5   4   3   2   1

Library of Congress Cataloging-in-Publication Data
is available from the publisher.

This book is available at quantity discounts for bulk purchases.
For information, please call 1-800-289-0963.

ACKNOWLEDGMENTS

On page 200 of this very book we advise authors to avoid overkill on their acknowledgment pages. "Try to avoid thanking . . . your second-grade teacher, the guy who sold you all those lattes, your cat," we primly counsel. Well, that's easier said than done.

First, a big shout-out to the Author Enabler Enablers: agent Deb Warren and the team at Adams Media, including Brendan O'Neill, Meredith O'Hayre, Ashley Vierra, Casey Ebert, Karen Cooper, Beth Gissinger, and Chelsea King. Thanks to Lynn Green and all our pals at BookPage for permission to use Author Enabler column excerpts, and to the intelligent and talented readers of our column and blog for asking questions that inspire us to learn. Thank you to Laina Adler, Eric Brandt, and Gideon Weil for their sage advice; to Betty Kamen for editorial help on the home front; and to Rabih Alameddine, Leslie Levine, Susanne Pari, and Amy Tan for brainstorming titles when we know they had other important work to do. We thank all the authors who contributed words of wisdom and experience, with special appreciation to Maya Angelou for both her foreword and her friendship.

Love and thanks to our amazing kids and their equally amazing sweethearts: Tony and Marissa Goldmark, Laura Barry, Daniel Barry, and Dilek Uygül. We also thank all the folks at HarperOne, West Coast Live, and the Friends of the San Francisco Public Library for working with us; and the Rock Bottom Remainders for playing with us. Then there's the guy who sold us all those lattes, not to mention his cat . . .

KATHI KAMEN GOLDMARK
and SAM BARRY

CONTENTS

FOREWORD

Nathaniel Hawthorne is credited with having said that easy reading is damned hard writing. I believe that, and also believe that easy writing may be damned hard reading. Kathi Kamen Goldmark and Sam Barry, both writers and wits, have given us a book called *Write That Book Already!*, which informs us about the ins and outs of writing for publication.

Obviously they agreed with Nathaniel Hawthorne, for while they are offering their book, and it is easy reading, in no way does it lead us to believe that writing for publication will be easy or easily achievable. Their writing is light and amusing. However, they remind the reader that if writing well is the goal, then time and patience and focus must be used in abundance.

I admire this book for its honesty, its bravery, and for its charm. Had I not decided, over forty years ago, to be a writer, I might have read this book and decided not to try. However, the joy they promise in their prose makes me glad that I and other writers have been willing to make good writing our aim, and even great writing our dream.

~Maya Angelou

ASK THE AUTHOR ENABLERS

They call to you from the store window. They also call from the library, your lover's bedside table, your friend's fanny pack, or your great-aunt's dusty attic. They lure you away from your housework, schoolwork, job, or career. They offer escape, entertainment, knowledge, enlightenment, humor, and the wisdom of the ages, in addition to their own unique brand of nourishment.

Of course, we're talking about that half-empty bag of fried pork rinds (your great-aunt's favorite, and her demise). But if you look in the other store, the bookstore, you'll see another kind of sustenance—the kind you find in books: the ones you love, the ones you read over and over again, the ones you've always meant to read and never got around to, and most especially, the one you plan to write.

As the Author Enablers, we get questions from aspiring writers from all over the world. There are those who think they have a book in them but who have no idea how to write. We often suggest to this group that they consider pursuing a more suitable and lucrative career, such as government lobbyist or investment banker. But most of the time we get interesting questions from a diverse group of people. Many of these folks are gifted writers who are struggling with the business end of publishing; others have a handle on marketing but find the writing to be tough. And there are many variations and combinations of these issues presenting a block to a writer's dream of becoming a published author. The most common question we get is some variation of "How do I get my book published?"

We intend to spend the rest of this book answering that question.

Along the way, we hope to demystify the overall writing and book-publishing process, revealing what happens to your book, step by step, between that first lightning-bolt of inspiration and the last ride to the shredder—oops, we mean the bestseller list. We'll also dispense plenty of good advice and tough-love reality checks, including the reminder that talent, luck, and timing all come into play. Our goal is to help you become one of the lucky, hard-working writers who wind up with a publishing contract.

But while we will focus on making the writing and publishing business clearer for all you aspiring authors, throughout this book we never want to forget to encourage you—whether or not you ever get a book published—to keep writing. Writing helps clarify thoughts and feelings, and being a good writer is essential to good communication skills, which will help you in every area of your life. Well, not in your golf game, and come to think of it not so much in your cooking or household chores. But writing is a good skill to have.

If your goal is to write a book for publication, rule number one is that no one ever finished a book without sitting down and getting started. Few authors get published without engaging in the daily discipline of writing, even if some days that means staring down a blank notebook or computer screen and drooling into your bag of pork rinds.

So fire up that laptop (or desktop, or Blackberry, or spiral note-book), apply butt to chair, and let's get started.

WHY WE WRITE (AND WHY YOU WRITE, TOO)

We all have stories to tell and important information to share. Whether or not you ever get published, the discipline of putting your words down on paper and improving your writing skills is good for you. Really.

Unlike the order in which most people read books, it happens that we are writing this first chapter last. The reason for this is that we've gone back and forth and back and forth again over the issues of voice and tone. On one hand, we want to present our writing to you in a consistent shared voice, much as we do in our *BookPage* column. That means taking a lighthearted tone and cracking a few jokes, while imparting useful information about writing and publishing.

On the other hand, if you've picked up this book then we know you are serious about your writing. And when we started writing Chapter 1 (the most important chapter in any book) we found ourselves getting pretty serious ourselves—even, dare we say it, a little preachy. We just couldn't help it. We care that much. But we don't want you to think we've lost our sense of humor.

What to do? At Author Enablers World Headquarters we aim to please. So here are two Chapter 1s: one is more lighthearted, one more sincere.

CHAPTER 1 (LITE)

Writing is an extension of something that is deeply ingrained in the human species—graffiti. Look at all those cave paintings! And those Egyptian tombs. Graffiti satisfies the age-old irrepressible urge to make one's indelible mark on a nice clean wall (or tomb). Writing helps us record history and empathize with others, even when we know those others are misguided and wrong. Just as we learn to walk, talk, and eat (anyone for pork rinds?), we learn to write by growing up around other people who write mysterious things we long to understand.

THE STORY OF WRITING

The earliest form of writing can be dated to around 3000 B.C., when the ancient Chinese discovered that they could keep secrets from their children by spelling words instead of saying them out loud. But many ancient cultures continued to pass on their knowledge, stories, and history by word of mouth. It took their bards and druids decades to learn everything they had to remember, and often by the time they had completed the task no one cared any more. Homer tried to keep things interesting with tales of food, violence, and loose women, which is why his stories are still being made into major motion pictures to this very day.

In general, as there was an increasing amount of history to remember, it became more efficient to write things down. But as time went on, cuneiform images and early alphabets became disfigured by natural erosion and graffiti artists, and—slowly and gradually—began to take on different meanings from one century to the next, resembling a very slow version of the children's game of Telephone. When the game begins, the first player must whisper a particular phrase into the next player's ear, but by the time the message gets to the end of the line, an amazing transformation may occur—a transformation so dramatic and bizarre that everyone is astonished! This was, in fact, how T. S. Eliot's poem *The Waste Land* was composed by a classroom of Irish kindergartners.

But we digress.

"What," we can hear you asking, "does an Irish kindergarten class or cuneiform graffiti have to do with me? I'm writing an important book about (pick as many as apply):

- Ethel Merman's costume jewelry and its cultural and historical importance
- Traveling with your pet goat
- The history of the lug wrench
- An alternate universe in which anyone who can't play the kazoo is imprisoned and tortured."

Whatever your subject, you believe the world needs to hear your message. You are certain that once the agents, editors, publishers, and movie producers of the world have access to your work, they will make you famous and offer you life-changing opportunities because you are *that good.*

"Come on, Author Enablers," you say, "show me the money."

Which shows how much you know—we don't have the money. The banks have the money. Still, whatever your message, writing makes it possible to compose and record your thoughts and stories in a form that will last as long as language is understood. And giving a little thought to why you want and need to write is a good idea.

CHAPTER 1 (SINCERE)

Writing is an extension of something that is deeply ingrained in the human species—language. Writing helps us clarify our thoughts and record history; it deepens our understanding of the world and allows us to empathize with others. We learn to speak when we're very young, and we use language to address almost every area of our lives. We use words to teach our children the lessons of life, to express emotion, to conduct commerce, to record our deepest religious practices, to share our knowledge, to stay connected, and to express the thoughts and ideas that emerge from our imaginations. Words are so important to us, so vital to our beings, that we sometimes take this gift of ours for granted. We shouldn't—words are too powerful to take for granted.

THE DIFFERENCE BETWEEN SCRIBBLING AND BABBLING

Connected though they are, spoken and written languages are very different. If you have ever written a speech, you may have learned this. A speechwriter must be conscious of the cadences of oratory, of course—you want to keep the audience engaged, or at least awake. But a speechwriter must also be aware that in the spoken word, the listener doesn't have the luxury of re-reading a difficult idea. This is why speechwriters often employ very straightforward language. People's minds may wander, and any audience will have represented in its ranks various levels of sophistication. To address these factors speechwriters use tricks such as repetition, or three simple points, or one example that is returned to again and again like a touchstone, which enables the listeners to make connections and follow the message.

Writers use similar tricks, and some tricks of the spoken word may help us to be better writers. However, because the reader has more time to review, consider, and mull over the message or story, the writer has far greater leeway to convey a more complex, nuanced message. But tone of voice and body language, essential tools of the spoken word, are missing on the page, which means the writer must work harder to convey the emotional content and intent of the message.

YOU HAVE TO READ TO WRITE—RIGHT? WRITE!

Most of us write because we read. Reading teaches us the power of words, of stories and history and argument. So, first and foremost, to be a writer you must be a reader. If you're like us you grew up reading everything—novels, history, popular science books, newspapers, comic books, cereal boxes, road signs—anything that was put in front of you. Just as we learn how to walk and talk, we learn how to write from others, from the people who go before us telling stories and recording history and trying to explain the meaning of it all. We read to get our vocabulary—not just the nouns and verbs and prepositions, but the means to express our mind, heart, and soul.

A crucial stage in any writer's development occurs long before the dream of writing a published book, at the moment when we go from reading to doing a bit of our own writing. This may happen when we are very young. It may be because we are not allowed to play with a toy until we've written a thank-you note, or we are given a notebook of some kind at school. Many of us will scrawl something almost illegible, but that illegible scrawl is the beginning of a moment of amazing discovery—the power of creating our own written words.

WHY WE WRITE

We write to tell a story, to describe an event, to imagine or explain what has been or will happen, to warn or touch or inspire. We write to express our most profound emotions—love and hatred, joy and sorrow, humor and sadness.

Writing is also how we pass on knowledge. This is why reading other writers is so important: by exploring the written works of the past we can perform a sort of archaeological dig, discovering how an idea has changed or persisted over thousands of years. Our ancestors speak to us through writing more directly than through any other medium, with the possible exception of YouTube.

Writing makes it possible for us to compose and record our thoughts and stories in a form that will last as long as the language is understood. The written word is fixed. Depending on what it is written with and on, the word can remain preserved for a very long time, and although a piece of writing can be interpreted in different ways, the text itself does not change—unless, of course, it is revised.

Writing is one of the most important, useful, and most rewarding of human endeavors. But you need to be disciplined and keep at it. Over time, you will be surprised by how much you accomplish.

BOTTOM LINE

You must sit down and write. Not *talk* about writing, but actual pen-to-paper or fingers-to-keyboard writing. Books are crafted one good sentence at a time. No matter what happens, if you persist, you won't be sorry. Human beings have been telling stories and discovering more about life and the world and passing it along via the written word for centuries. You are part of that tradition. Be humble, but also be proud.

CHAPTER TWO

YOU HAVE A GREAT IDEA. SO WHAT?

Okay, so maybe you are the world's authority on the art of making butter sculptures of dead presidents' heads, but if you want to sell a book on the subject you'll have to do more than know your stuff. You'll need to make the idea sound sexy, or cool, or hot, or timely, or cute, or something that instantly makes it clear to people why the world needs your book.

When it comes down to it, you, the author, are trying to talk total strangers into investing their time, effort, and money in you and your idea. You need to sell yourself to the agents of the world so they in turn can sell you to the acquiring editors, who will sell to the publishers, whose marketing team will sell to the sales force, who will sell to the book buyers of stores and other retailers, who will sell to their staff, who will sell to the public. There are other models but the point is that (in case we aren't making ourselves clear) you'll need to sell yourself and your idea again and again throughout the process.

MINING FOR GOLD

Along the way everything will get refined, and in the process your book may even morph into something else. Your title may change (actually, this is likely to happen), a subtitle may get added, and the manuscript will need revision—perhaps even a major overhaul. The one-liner "elevator pitch" that you came up with to describe the book may become an altogether different one-liner. The changes will keep coming.

This may be disconcerting, but we suggest that you approach all the roughhouse this way: instead of thinking, "I am the author, and this is my book—what do these people know?" try to think, "This is exciting—people are interested enough in me and my book to invest their time and energy into making it more salable." This doesn't mean you can't fight for what you believe in, especially if it comes down to the integrity of your book or your own core beliefs. But stay loose and open—some of the ideas that are suggested to you may be improvements.

A TRUE-LIFE EXAMPLE TO ILLUSTRATE OUR POINT

For example (just to pull an example out of the air), let's say you've come up with an idea for a combination inspiration/humor book that teaches the reader how to become more playful in life via learning to play the harmonica. It's a unique idea, but when you describe it to publishing professionals the first comparison title that seems to come to mind is *Zen and the Art of Motorcycle Maintenance,* and despite the fact that neither you nor anyone else you've talked to about your idea has ever actually read *Zen and the Art of Motorcycle Maintenance,* it is a well-known, strong-selling book with a recognizable title that pairs an odd combination of concepts. In other words, your book is a little weird, but so is *Zen and the Art of Motorcycle Maintenance*, and it sold a ton of copies, so maybe yours will too!

Your book, *How to Play,* is sold to a small publisher of elegant design books and earthy humor books, and you are introduced to your editor via e-mail. The editor likes the humor aspects of your book, and asks you to beef them up, so you do. Then she asks for major cuts in word count, so that your manuscript will conform to a required design template. Many of these cuts make good sense—and will make for a stronger book. You get rid of some redundancies and the weaker jokes, but there are a few suggested cuts you simply don't want to make. This is an instance where choosing your battles will stand you in good stead. If you've been a good sport about making changes that weren't crucial to you, you'll have more credibility when you stand up for the passages you feel are essential, like the passage where you quote John Belushi saying "I owe it all to little chocolate donuts." Who wouldn't fight for keeping *that* in their book?

YOU CAN'T MAKE A SILK PURSE FROM A SOW'S EAR

Getting back to all that selling—the publisher needs to start with good materials. The first and most important matter is a ship-shape manuscript, or a good proposal if you are writing nonfiction (including at least part of a well-written manuscript). Next, research the market for your book. Don't take this task lightly—it will benefit everyone to know what else is out there. This research will tell you what's selling now or recently that is similar, and how your book is unique—if it is.

Don't be afraid to face the fact that someone else may have already successfully done what you are attempting to do. This may mean you need to rethink your idea, or even throw it out. It also may mean that there is a huge market for your kind of book, in which case you are planning to jump on the bandwagon and aren't that concerned with originality. Perhaps you can tweak your idea just enough to say, "See, this is new and different!" even though it really isn't all that unique. Putting a new spin on a comfortably familiar idea is something that is done all the time. Originality is a complex concept and we are not going to attempt to wrestle it to the ground here. Suffice it to say, each book is a different case. At times it seems as if there is nothing new under the sun, so don't worry about it, just invent a better mousetrap (and, if you correctly guess the number of clichés in this paragraph, our hats are off to you). From another perspective: each book and author is unique, and you don't need to try too hard to be the first, the only, and so on—you already are an original. Just keep your mind open to what the world needs and watch for your niche.

Tough Love from the Author Enablers

Do you want to be a published author, or did you really just write this book for yourself or your own private audience? Now's the time to decide, because once you engage an agent and sell to a publisher your book isn't solely yours anymore. ‹ «

Your editor works with you on your manuscript changes, and then springs another surprise: the sales reps don't think the title *How to Play* will be easy to sell to their accounts, and they want to change the title to something you aren't sure works. At this point, it might be prudent to get your agent involved, so she can act as the "bad cop" and insist that more thinking go into the title question, or title/subtitle question if your book is nonfiction—remembering, of course, that your contract likely stipulates that the publisher does indeed have the right to change the title and design the cover as well, not to mention change your name if they don't like it. No, just kidding about the name thing. We have never heard of a publisher ever insisting on such an outrageous demand. Suggesting, maybe, even strongly. Perhaps misspelling your name on the book jacket by mistake. But never actually telling you to change your name. Really. Who would do such a thing? Hollywood, maybe, but not a book publisher.

A compromise is finally reached, and *How to Play* has become *How to Play the Harmonica: and Other Life Lessons*. There's a lot less harmonica and inspiration, a lot more humor. The cover is catchy, and while you worry that it might not capture your original vision . . . well, they may be right and you may be wrong. Who knows? *How to Play the Harmonica: and Other Life Lessons* just might jump off the shelves into the arms of cager impulse buyers. You do need the force to be with you—the sales force, that is—and this is the title they ultimately agreed they could do the best job of selling.

DO YOUR HOMEWORK (BEFORE YOU GO OUT TO PLAY)

Researching the competition and market can take some time. It is easy to go to the websites of online retailers and get a snapshot of what's selling now. Amazon and Barnes & Noble both offer search mechanisms and sales rankings, and take our word for it, professionals in publishing use these sites all the time for their own research and to keep an eye on market trends. Publishing professionals are aware that Amazon ranking can be misleading. The ranking is affected by how often the title is searched (and not necessarily sold), and does not reflect sales in other retail outlets. You should also visit a variety of bookstores to see how books are displayed, and which titles are front and center. Talk to the bookstore employees, especially those who seem more experienced, and ask them which titles, similar to yours, they might recommend—and how well those books are selling. Go to your library and do a similar exercise. Make a list of the competitive titles, including author, publisher, publication date, and whether the book hit any bestseller lists or won awards, and write a brief description, focusing on those from recent years and including a few classics of the genre. Read some reviews for these books (these can be found online). Remember, all this research will make you a more knowledgeable, savvy author, and will equip you for making your pitch—and for writing a better book.

Determining accurate sales numbers for the competition titles is harder. Publishers don't generally reveal these numbers, except when they want to brag ("More than one million copies sold!"). There are services that provide this information for the industry, but it isn't the author's job to provide sales numbers in detail—you have enough other work to do. If you do the research above you should have a good sense of which titles succeeded and to what degree, and your agent or the editor can fill in the details.

A SUCCESSFUL CAMPAIGN NEEDS A SOLID PLATFORM

Aside from the competitive research and your daily writing, you can be laying the groundwork for your platform. "Platform" is a term used to define the group of people who know who you are and care about what you have to say, starting with your mother. Platforms are as varied as the authors who are standing on them. Some people develop a platform first, by being experts in fields that make them of interest as public speakers or writers. Perhaps they write articles in newspapers, in magazines, online, or all of the above. Perhaps they go before audiences and speak. Maybe they get on radio or television. Maybe they blog or tweet to thousands, or send out a monthly newsletter. Maybe they do some combination of all or some of these.

If you think about it, this kind of a platform can apply to any number of situations. A popular minister or rabbi can have a platform. So can a teacher or professor, or a health professional or healer, or a martial artist, or a motivational speaker, politician, artist (performing or otherwise), athlete, soldier, astronaut, mother of twenty-two, business person, clown, or horse whisperer. But the list is not limited to people in reputable fields—actors, con artists, people in prison, people who should be in prison, and other shady characters may develop platforms because their stories are unique or they are great salespeople, writers, or speakers. (Concerning the latter two, Sam's brother Dave comes to mind.) Additionally, a person may have experienced a personal tragedy or overcome adversity and become a spokesperson for a particular cause or issue. The point is, this is someone with something to say that the world wants to hear.

FICTION WRITERS AND PLATFORM

Fiction writers, don't despair—we know this all sounds like it applies only to the world of nonfiction. And to some degree it does. Your primary job as a fiction writer is to create a good book by the standards of your genre—lots of beautiful sentences with a convoluted, hard-to-follow plot if you are shooting for literary fiction, two dead people and a tough hero character established by page three if you are writing a thriller, a likeable, spunky female character looking for (and finding) a great guy if you are writing a romance (you've got to throw in an evil but sexy vampire if you are writing a vampire romance), and so on. You know your genre, or you should. Of course we kid about the stereotypes. No one writes according to such simplistic formulas! Well, yes, they do, but the ones who succeed know how to tell a great story and are exceptional at what they do—and some even invented the formula.

But getting back to fiction writers and platform—the best thing you can do is get some of your writing out there into the world. Write short fiction and get it published anywhere you can. Go to writers' workshops if you can afford the time and tuition. Teach writing if that makes sense for you. See if you can get a short piece of yours published online or read on the radio. Write topical pieces about unique experiences in your life. It's okay to cross over and do a little nonfiction writing—good writing is good writing, and getting published or noticed in any way can't hurt your career.

For you nonfiction writers, the path to building a platform is clearer but also more demanding, because the expectations are higher. Publishers want to know that you already have something going. So here are some ways to get started.

BUILDING YOUR PLATFORM, ONE PERSON AT A TIME

Believe it or not, you can develop fans one person at a time. (Sam has, personally, developed fourteen fans in his life, though not for himself.) Let's say you do a lot of public speaking about the benefits of green kamut for maintaining digestive health, but the crowds are small. Make some appealing business cards or small flyers and make sure you have a few on hand (in your purse, car, briefcase, pocket, underwear) at all times. Don't be obnoxious about forcing them on people, but the next time you're sitting on an airplane and overhear your seatmate burp repeatedly and say "Gosh, I wish I knew more about how to maintain my digestive health," it's the perfect opportunity for you to whip out your card and promote your product and yourself . . . *and* you might end up with a new stalker! You'll recognize your fan when you pick up the phone and the heavy breathing is interrupted by burps. Here are some more ways to build your platform:

Maintain a good e-mail/mailing list, but don't spam people. There are some wonderful web-based programs (for instance, Constant Contact) set up for maintaining and communicating with large groups of people. Many feature protocols that allow fans to sign themselves up via your website, and also let you import lists of contacts from other programs. Make sure you add only people who want to be on your list, and don't drive your contacts crazy with too many e-mail blasts. Let people know how often they can expect to hear from you (once a week? once a month? every five minutes?) and expect "opt-outs" when you send more than the expected number of e-mails. Remember that everyone is busy. We all get too much e-mail, and it is an honor to be selected by the folks who sign up for your list, no matter how important you think you are. Don't abuse the privilege, like Sam did with those fourteen people.

Start your own website, blog, Twitter, Fwix, YouTube account, Facebook page, and so on. By the time this book is in your hands, there will no doubt be many more social-networking arenas. Do whatever you can to keep up, including (gack!) actually learning about this stuff. Having a fourteen-year-old in your life can be enormously helpful.

Pursue online publication. Online magazines and journals, which go by various names such as e-zines and e-journals, won't necessarily pay much (though some are fair in their compensation), but if you have patience and a fresh, flexible, and innovative approach, these publications can provide you with opportunities to get your work seen. As with traditional magazines, many of these sites cater to specific interests and audiences, such as health needs, new parents, and so on. This is a new medium requiring patience and flexibility, because it is almost certain to keep growing and evolving in the years to come.

Seek out public speaking and teaching opportunities. Is there something you know how to do that others want to learn? Even if it has nothing to do with your book, offering your expertise in a classroom or public-speaking setting will help you get accustomed to "performing" when the time comes to read from your Pulitzer-Prize-winning novel, and that day you read the wrong e-mail and showed up at your child's middle-school career day in your chicken costume instead of your nurse's uniform could end up providing some great material for future books. No venue or group is too humble a place to start, and if you turn out to be a talented communicator you might be surprised at the results. If you are patient, over time people will come to know your name and seek you out.

Write for (and to) newspapers and magazines. Max Ebb is a beloved columnist in *Latitude 38,* a monthly magazine that is popular with sailboat enthusiasts. Chances are, if you don't sail you have never heard of Max, but if you happen to mention that you are his sister or brother-in-law (so we've heard) you will be treated like royalty at any yacht club bar in the San Francisco Bay Area. Max's column is funny and well-written while dispensing clearheaded advice about sailboat racing. Max got his start at *Latitude 38* by writing hilarious (and frequent) letters to the editor. The editor liked his writing so much that he placed an ad in his own magazine asking Max to get in touch so he could get paid for his writing. This was almost thirty years ago, and Max is still not only writing his monthly column but also now threatening to turn his columns into a book. You might not be as lucky as Max, but writing letters to the editor (or posting on popular blogs) is one way to get noticed by the powers that be at a publication. Another way is to research the submission guidelines and craft a terrific pitch letter. Make sure you are familiar enough with the magazine (including content, word count of articles, writing style, and audience demographic) to pitch appropriately. Max didn't write brilliant letters about sailboat racing to *Knitting Journal* or *Pizza Today*, and neither should you.

Present yourself as an expert to radio and television producers. Are you an expert on the nonverbal communication patterns of African gorillas? Make sure the producers of your local radio and TV stations' news shows are aware of this fact. Send a one-sheet press release (to the shows, not the gorillas) listing your credentials and contact information and ask to be put on the "expert list." Then, the next time a new community of gorillas is discovered in an African jungle, they just might give you a call. Try to get a recording of your interview or appearance, and add it to your list of credentials for next time.

Do you sense a theme here? You need to be graciously self-promoting. Use your best manners, but don't be shy and always be prepared with information at the ready when needed. Once again, no journal, newspaper, classroom, church group, website, blog, publication, or band of gorillas is too small to be worth your time when you're starting out, and success will lead to more success. Eventually you'll have achieved the ever-elusive and mysterious state of being: you'll be a writer with a platform. No kidding.

FICTION VERSUS NONFICTION VERSUS MEMOIR

Are the rules different for different kinds of books? You bet they are. The submission guidelines vary considerably for fiction, nonfiction, poetry, and children's books. But don't be discouraged or frightened of the proposal-writing and submission process—once you settle in and start doing the work it really isn't so bad. You need to be clear on what it is you are writing—and be prepared to patiently explain this over and over again. The rest of the world isn't always paying attention.

YOU'VE JUST COMPLETED THE GREAT AMERICAN (OR CANADIAN, OR WHATEVER) NOVEL

The scene: a festive holiday gathering. You walk in, feeling spectacular. In the year since you've last seen the host of the party you've sold your first novel. Because these are shallow, physique-obsessed times, you've also worked your butt off (literally) to lose thirty pounds—or, if you are a guy, to develop those "six pack" abs (and if you are a guy, you have failed) and spent a chunk of your sizable book advance on the stunning designer outfit you're wearing (or, if you are a guy, you sprang for a new belt and a haircut).

Tough Love from the Author Enablers

So—are you making this stuff up, or is it cold, hard truth? You'd better know the difference, and learn the rules for submitting your type of manuscript. ‹ ‹‹

You're ready to take on the world. The room is filled mostly with strangers . . . but there, holding court between the stuffed olives and the green-tea punch, you see a familiar face: Swarthmore DuLuc, wearing a festive seasonal tie and red-and-green slacks, a likeable acquaintance you run into only once a year at this event. You make a beeline for old Swarthmore because he will be good for at least ten minutes of conversation while you get your bearings.

If you are a woman (or a man who is in touch with his feminine side), the conversation might go a little like this:

You: Hey, happy holidays.

SD: Same to you, dear—(kisses on both cheeks)—and don't you look smashing! Have we lost weight?

You: Oh, maybe a pound or two.

SD: And *who* are we wearing this season?

You: This old thing? Just something I found in the back of the closet.

SD: Well, you do look fetching. Tell me, my little kumquat, what have we been up to this year?

If you are a man, (or a woman in touch with her inner linebacker), it might go this way:

You: Yo, Dude.

SD: Whoa, what happened to you? You been sick or something?

You (wondering if your new belt is doing a better job of holding in your paunch): Nah, I just dropped a couple of pounds. Did you catch the game last night?

SD (sneering): I don't watch spectator sports. Squash is my game. I haven't seen you around lately—what have you been up to?

You (seizing the opportunity to talk about your book): Actually, I have some terrific news. I sold a novel and it's going to be published in the spring. I'm very excited.

SD: That's wonderful! I couldn't be happier for you—your first published novel. What's it about? Is it fiction or nonfiction?

Aside from the fact that you can't tell if old Swarthy is really happy for you, you'd be surprised how many people, including many of the aspiring writers who contact us at Author Enablers World Headquarters, don't know what genre they are writing in. For instance, many people don't understand that a novel—by definition—is a work of fiction. Or at least it's supposed to be. Deciding on the genre of your book (fiction, nonfiction, memoir, children's book, etc.) is important for many reasons: it will determine how the book is edited, designed, marketed, and sold.

READ THE INSTRUCTIONS: SUBMISSION GUIDELINES FOR DIFFERENT GENRES

You wouldn't use a power tool without first reading the manual, would you? Why should preparing your proposal be any different? Although there are always exceptions (the stories about seven-figure advances given for one-page sample chapters come to mind), here are the general guidelines for submitting a manuscript.

SUBMITTING FICTION

A work of fiction can be a full-length novel, a novella, a short story, even a poem (Vikram Seth wrote his first novel, *The Golden Gate,* completely in sonnet verse to avoid completing his Stanford graduate thesis in economics. Way to go, Vikram! We avoided our theses, too, though they weren't in economics. Kathi avoided hers by writing novelty folk songs, while Sam focused on playing the harmonica, with breaks for ping pong and learning trick Frisbee throws.) Fiction's first and foremost rule is that the work is made up, rather than history or fact. This doesn't mean that you can't draw from real experience or memory. It does mean that you get to use your imagination and create any story you want to.

When submitting a work of fiction, especially if it's your first, you should have your entire manuscript completed and at least informally copyedited. Also include a story synopsis—the process of creating a synopsis may help clarify your pitch and even improve the novel itself. You'll need to include biographical materials, and this is the time to make yourself sound as accomplished and well-known as you honestly can.

It will help your cause if you include some preliminary marketing materials:

- A list of your other published works, if any
- Comparison titles, meaning novels like yours (but not *too* much like yours) that have sold well
- Any endorsements you've managed to solicit from published authors or prominent figures, and/or a truthful list of potential blurbers
- If possible, some marketing information about your "platform," or public fan base

Make sure your contact information is accurate and visible on every appropriate page.

But mostly, with fiction, you want to put your best foot forward with terrific writing and unforgettable characters engaged in an original, imaginative story. Piece o' cake, right? We do it every day, in between playing catch with the old Frisbee while playing the harmonica.

SUBMITTING NONFICTION

A work of nonfiction tells a real story of events that actually happened. Nonfiction includes history, current events, parenting, business, memoirs, self-help, how-to, cookbooks, and so on. Nonfiction is stuff you don't make up (and we've all heard the stories of those who've tried to pass off fiction as nonfiction).

Here are some general guideline submissions for a nonfiction manuscript from Eric Brandt, who works as a senior editor for HarperCollins Publishers. (Thanks, Eric!) These are not rules, just suggestions from a pro who looks at a lot of book proposals:

What to Include in Your Proposal

1. **One sentence description of your book (often called the keynote or hook)**

   "Muslim-American female reporter goes undercover on the Hajj to Mecca to discover the changing role of women in Islam."

   "Excommunicated monk finds love and spiritual redemption in the arms of a Las Vegas showgirl."

   "In time for the America's Cup, award-winning novelist tells story of obsessed sea captain who defies Greenpeace to hunt albino whale."

   If you can't reduce your book to one sentence, you may not have a clear thesis. According to *Bowker,* the global provider of book information, 291,000 new books were published in the United States in 2006. That flood of titles doesn't leave a lot of time for a publisher's sales rep to "sell" your book to bookstores, libraries, and other retailers. Give your potential publisher a compelling hook to grab attention and get the gist of your book.

2. **A one- to two-page description of your book**
3. **Table of contents (TOC)**
4. **Detailed outline (ten pages)**
5. **Sample chapter**
6. **Competition and related titles**—tell how each of these succeeded (meaning the subject is of interest to the world) but has also fallen short, and how your book will not only differ from but also be better than these other books.

   Here it is okay to say things like "My biography of Rush Limbaugh will be scandalous like Kitty Kelley's *The Family: The Real Story of the Bush Dynasty,* but funny like Al Franken's *Lies and the Lying Liars Who Tell Them: A Fair and Balanced Look at the Right.*"

Or

"My self-help book combines the Christian inspirational impact and programmatic approach of Rick Warren's blockbuster hit *The Purpose Driven Life* with the prurient satisfaction of Jenna Jameson's autobiography, *How to Make Love Like a Porn Star.*"

7. **Market or audience for your book:**
"Readers of Dan Brown or Doris Kearns Goodwin"

"Expectant mothers and fathers"

"Dog-loving vampires"

"Vampire-loving dogs"

"College-educated retirees concerned about rising medical costs"

"Urban Gen-X professionals"

"Frisbee-throwing harmonica enthusiasts"

8. **Promotion and publicity suggestions**
What can you do to help publicize your book once published? Do you have a website? blog? list of e-mail addresses of people interested in your topic? Do you have connections to relevant organizations (MADD, Young Democrats, NRA, American Cancer Society, etc.)? Do you speak in public? Where and how often? Any connections in the media?

9. **Length and estimated completion date of manuscript**
Approximately how many thousands of words will your book be? 50,000 words is a shorter nonfiction adult book. Short is not necessarily bad, and can in fact be a selling point—it depends on the material. You're not being paid

by the word, and a huge manuscript can be a sign that you don't know how to self-edit your work. On the other hand, your subject matter may call for length, e.g., *Everything You Ever Wanted to Know about Elvis, Marilyn Monroe, James Dean, the Beatles, Michael Jackson, and Britney Spears.*

10. **Author bio/credentials**
Education, professional and other experience, awards, residence. Make sure your contact information is accurate and visible on every appropriate page.

Most agents and publishers list their proposal requirements on their websites. Make sure you submit according to the specific guidelines given.

When you're submitting proposals for cookbooks and how-to books, along with your sample chapter you'll need to include some recipes or other examples of whatever it is you are teaching. Be certain that you have tested your processes and are confident that they really work and won't hurt anyone, and that people will understand your instructions.

Submissions for children's books usually require the entire manuscript (which sometimes amounts to very few words). In general you can expect to send a query letter and the full manuscript text for picture books, and a query letter and a few prints or jpegs of children and animals if you are including illustrations. Keep in mind that many publishers will want to do their own matchmaking when it comes to children's book text and illustrations. You won't necessarily get to choose your own illustrator, especially on a first book.

If you're submitting poetry, most editors expect a complete or significantly complete manuscript, a publication history for poems that have appeared in literary magazines, and any background information or personal experience that could help in selling the

book (associations, teaching positions, past public readings etc.).
Oh, and good poems.

Tough Love from the Author Enablers

With all submissions, it's important that you see the agent's or
publisher's website or listing in Literary Market Place for submission guidelines—these folks get a lot of spam and lunatics
sending stuff their way. And we wouldn't advise sending the
same query to several different agents at the same agency or
editors at a publishing house. As always, remember to enclose
a contact phone number as well as your e-mail address. ‹ «

A memoir is a story, often told in the first person, of events that
have occurred in the writer's life. Memoir is officially defined as nonfiction, but gets its own special category here because readers of memoirs
also tend to be fiction readers. Memoir style can run the gamut from
self-help and inspiration to the highest form of literary prose—and
includes everything in between. If you're planning to write a memoir,
be sure to keep it real. There have been incidents of writers passing off
fiction as memoir, resulting in embarrassment, distrust, and (sometimes) humongous book sales. But don't count on that working for
you. Long-term, it's better to hold on to your integrity and to be clear
and honest about what you are offering to the world.

WAITING FOR THE MAIL: RESPONSE TIME AND DEALING WITH REJECTION

Remember, agents and editors are busy people who receive a
large volume of submissions. Allow at least a month or two for them
to read and respond to your submission—often it takes longer.

Be professional and courteous in your approach to any agent.
Agents do form an impression based on your query letter, and you
want it to be a good impression. Take the time to write a focused,
well-constructed, and succinct letter, and—have we said this enough

times?—follow any guidelines provided. Proofread approximately 400 times, to catch and eliminate errors, before sending.

Unfortunately, publishing is a business that involves a lot of rejection, at every stage. Despite how it might appear, agents and publishers don't delight in saying "no"—they are as eager to find great ideas and great writing as you are to be published. But agents can only represent a small fraction of the authors out there; it's a simple reality. Agents and publishers reject manuscripts for many reasons—because of changing trends in the market; because they already have a similar book on their list or know of similar published or forthcoming titles; because something just doesn't feel like a good fit; or even because the right person read your proposal on the wrong day and didn't fall in love with it, even if it's strong, well-written, and publishable.

If an agent or editor says no thanks to your query, consider that no thanks to be from the agency or publisher as a whole—in other words, don't send your proposal to other editors or agents within the same publishing house or agency. And above all, try to keep "No" in perspective. This is a highly subjective business; all it takes is one "Yes."

BOTTOM LINE

You need to know what you are writing. Next, you need to read and follow all submission guidelines for the agents and publishers to whom you submit—and approach these folks with courtesy. There are many stories of authors who achieved their dreams after collecting a pile of rejections. If you get a rejection, don't give up. Our mothers called this "sticktoitiveness." It's a silly word for an important quality. Thomas Edison didn't give up. Eleanor Roosevelt didn't give up. Harriet Tubman didn't give up. David Golia didn't give up. Neither should you.

CHAPTER THREE

HOW TO GET STARTED WITH THE WRITE STUFF

If quick fame is what you're after, you might want to try reality TV. Don't choose writing as a vocation unless you really love it, can't help doing it, or have an important message that is best conveyed through the written word. For one thing, writing is hard work, not least because it involves a lot of actual writing.

It's unlikely that a publisher or agent will come along and say, "You look like a fascinating person with a great story to tell," although some guys will try and use this as a pickup line in bars. Most of the world's writers toil away privately, sometimes for years, before anyone tries to pick them up in a bar, or, for that matter, acknowledges their writing talents.

Reasons *not* to become a professional writer:
- You long for financial security.
- You crave the limelight.
- You need structure in your life.
- You want to have one secure, steady source of income.
- You like spending time with your family, friends, pets, hobbies, and other interests.
- You don't want to offend members of your family or friends and colleagues, who often think you are writing about them whether that is true or not (and let's be honest, you *are* often writing about them, and some of us may *want* to offend).
- You want to be of service to the world.
- You like hanging around trendy, well-dressed people.

Assuming that you do want to be a writer (because you're still reading this book), let's address some issues that may arise in the course of your career.

THE WELL OF LONELINESS VERSUS THE FORTRESS OF SOLITUDE

Writing is a solitary occupation. For some people this may be great news, but most of us need the inspiration and feedback that come from human interaction. Think about it: how do we learn what happened in our favorite television show last night, or who's going to win the big game this weekend? From our colleagues at work! And what about perfecting our skills in the competitive sport of shooting paper clips with a rubber band? How are you going to flirt with the receptionist if you work alone at home?

If you are a natural-born loner, the writing life will be very comfortable. But if, like most of us, you need the inspiration that comes from hitting someone in the back of the head with a paper clip while winking at the receptionist—not that we've ever behaved this way—then carving out focused time alone may be difficult and even uncomfortable.

Writers need solitude, but there is a world of difference between solitude and loneliness. From the outside they look alike, in that they involve being by yourself, but this surface resemblance doesn't tell the full story. When we are lonely we feel isolated—something is missing. We can even feel lonely when we are with people, like when we were picked last for teams on the playground in grade school (not that we're bitter).

Solitude, on the other hand, is being alone without being lonely. Solitude is what writers need—the time and space to be alone and still be able to provide themselves with satisfying company. Solitude doesn't require that you be physically alone—some people write in cafés, surrounded by the ambient noise of strangers. Others write at home with music playing, or with family life going on all around them. With portable computers or old-fashioned pen and paper you can write almost anywhere, and some writers are inspired by having a lively scene around them, such as a park or cityscape. Some writers share studio space. For instance, in San Francisco there is a collective of writers called the Grotto who maintain shared office space that also serves as a forum for professional, creative, and social interaction. (We've heard *their* paper clip fights are not only legendary, but also literary.)

GETTING INTO THE ZONE

Whatever works for you—and your preferences may evolve over time—the trick is getting your consciousness into a space that we call the Zone. The Zone is a creative state of mind in which the writing flows, much as it is flowing for us right now. You feel connected to your own imagination (is that Yanni we hear, softly playing in the background?), ideas flow, synapses connect, and before you know it you have filled the page—with drawings of airplanes and battleships! No, seriously, you've done some writing.

Many new writers make the mistake of thinking they have to feel the Zone before they begin to work, when more often it is the other way around: getting in the Zone comes from the act of writing. Yes, you should arrange for the right atmosphere (e.g., your study, the café, the Nordstrom shoe department, the bowling alley, the strip club). Just don't wait for some imagined, perfect moment. This is not a Hollywood movie where inspiration hits, the pages of the calendar start falling away, and you are suddenly a bestselling author. Start writing, and the muse will come. Not every time, but keep at it, and the muse will come enough for you to get the initial writing done.

In this sense writing is similar to exercise. For instance, many of us don't enjoy doing crunches. If we wait until we feel inspired to do that extra abdominal work, let's be honest, we'll do it about once a year, if that. But if we do it every day, we will look like a swimsuit model in a year. Or maybe a swimsuits model's dumpier big brother or sister. But the point is that we will be in better shape, and that never would have happened if we hadn't made ourselves get down on the floor to exercise every day, whether we felt like it or not. It is the same with writing—do it every day for a year, and you will look like a swimsuit model's sister or brother, *plus* you will have 300 pages of written material, some of it really good, that you can hone into a book. Writing is a discipline, and you have to stay at it. Inspiration will come.

One of the bonuses you'll get from the time you spend writing is that you'll feel like you're spending time with friends as you develop a relationship with the characters in your book, whether fictional or nonfictional. Kathi often worries about the characters in her novels, and what trouble they might be getting into when she's not with them. She even window shops for them, and has been known to ask for their advice in tough personal situations. That's what's called a creative mind. Oh, sure, there are other terms . . .

TIME MANAGEMENT

You wake up in the morning knowing that today's the day! You've planned carefully by taking time off work and arranging sleepovers for the kids. You shower and dress, make a pot of coffee, and boot up your computer. Nothing—absolutely nothing in the world—is going to keep you from finishing ten pages of your epic gourmet thriller, *Sous Chef in Hell's Kitchen— In the Soup*.

As your desktop loads, you remember last night's phone message from your sister. You make what you think will be a quick call, but end up hearing forty-five minutes of whining about your brother-in-law, who has—what can he be thinking?—decided to write a novel! Not only that, he says he needs to do a lot of his research in strip clubs. You say all the right supportive things, hang up as soon as you can, pour yourself another cup of coffee, and click on your document.

Tough Love from the Author Enablers

You will never be a writer if you don't write. ‹ «

Only thing is, the file won't open. You try rebooting but that doesn't work, so you end up calling the friend-of-a-friend who knows about computers. His phone line is disconnected so you open your Outlook program in order to send him an e-mail.

As your inbox fills, you find a couple of e-mails that really can't wait. You answer them efficiently, but by the time you realize that your message to Mr. Computer Guy has bounced back, you've cruised through the land of irresistible-jokes-that-you-have-to-send-to everyone and on to hilarious YouTube videos.

Okay, the computer guy has apparently skipped town with no forwarding address, but that doesn't mean you can't call tech support. After fifty-six minutes on hold, a $49 charge to your Visa, an hour on the phone with someone who knows less about computers than you do, and finally a reluctant transfer to "level 2 support," a nice young woman in Mumbai coaxes you through a system restore procedure that allows you to retrieve your manuscript. Sweating and jangled, nevertheless you make another pot of coffee and sit down to work.

The doorbell rings. It's your elderly neighbor, Eunice, complaining about your dog peeing on her rose bushes. You don't have a dog and she doesn't have any rose bushes, but you take the time to calm her down, and while you're outside you pick up the mail. There are a couple of bills, so you sign on to do some online banking, promising yourself you are going to do that writing any minute now.

The day goes on, delivering one interruption after another, until you look at the clock and see that it's time to pick up the kids and figure out what to do about dinner. Another promising writing day has gone down the tubes.

STUFF HAPPENS

Here's the thing: whatever your schedule, stuff is going to happen. People will make demands on your time, your equipment is going to fail, and your family and friends need you. The world is not going to roll over and make it easy for you to get your writing done. In fact, many people might try (either consciously or unconsciously) to sabotage your efforts. *You* may sabotage your efforts. That's the way it is for everyone—you're not alone.

Procrastination

You procrastinate when you put off things that you should be focusing on right now, usually in favor of doing something that is more enjoyable or that you're more comfortable doing. Here is a list of all the reasons not to sit down and write. You need to:

- Earn a living
- Do your homework
- Cook dinner
- Do some more research, including field trips, for that book you've been planning on writing for thirty years now
- Post on all your regular blogs
- Find a writing partner
- Play Scrabble to maintain the sharpness of your mind
- Floss
- Call Aunt Trudy
- Watch *The Price is Right*

Are you getting the idea? There are always a lot of other things to do besides write. The only problem is, none of them will make you a writer. We procrastinators (most of us) work just as long and hard as everyone else, but on the wrong goals. We may be failing to prioritize or we may be overwhelmed. Other causes of procrastination include waiting for the right mood or time to start, fear of failure or success, being disorganized or distracted, and perfectionism. Regardless of the cause, if we want to be writers, we need to focus. And be brave. And we probably also need to floss.

Some Time Management Strategies We Got Straight from the Pentagon:

- *Concentrate on results, not on being busy.* At the heart of good time management is this important shift in focus. Many people spend their days in a frenzy of activity, but achieve very little, or achieve lots of little things but not the one big goal. They're not concentrating their effort on what they claim matters most to them. If you keep putting off your writing, it is time to decide whether or not you really want to be a writer. You don't *have* to write, you know; there are many other satisfying and worthy vocations.

- *Make a to-do list.* If we've inspired you to start writing, great—but of course that means you probably aren't reading this paragraph. For the rest of us, maybe a few old-fashioned tricks will help achieve the goal. If you feel overwhelmed by the amount of work you have to do or keep being distracted from writing by other matters, perhaps a to-do list will help. But here's the thing—make sure you put the most important tasks at the top of the list and the least important at the bottom. And guess what the Author Enablers are going to say is the most important task? That's right—write.

- *Write down goals.* Set some clearly defined, reasonable goals, so you can measure your progress and take pride in the achievement of those goals. For instance, you might plan on writing two double-spaced pages every day. Stay with it and you'll be amazed at how quickly your manuscript will grow. This will raise your self-confidence. You should also set some bigger-picture goals: complete the first draft of your manuscript in a year, compile a list of agents two months later, write a query letter two weeks after that, world domination by your next birthday, get a dog and plant a rose bush for Eunice by the time you're fifty, and so on.

- *Establish a schedule.* It will also help to plan your time. You don't need a complicated schedule, but you need to set aside the time to write, if possible early in the day, so that you can then move on and deal with the rest of your list. If it helps you, make a schedule and follow it every day. Respect the to-do list and the schedule, take them seriously, and when you do screw up, get back on the horse immediately and write. We mean it. Not about the horse, but about not letting self-pity or fatigue or negative thinking keep you from sticking to a clear, simple regimen. If you fail to write Tuesday, write Wednesday and forget about Tuesday. If you only write half a page on Thursday, good, at least you tried—now write two pages on Friday. Keep at this discipline and eventually you will finish your manuscript. We promise.

AUTHOR CARE 101

There are various strategies when it comes to living the life of a writer. One is to drink yourself silly, ruin your body, and destroy all your most important relationships, as many great writers have done. Or you can take care of yourself. We suggest the latter course. Whatever is holding you back, it's time to get over it. This calls for full-tilt honesty on your part, without putting yourself down (another way we avoid writing—"I'm no good").

Start making those goals, keeping that list, and setting aside the time to write. When you fail, take a good look at why and refocus on your primary goal. If you find the writing to be disagreeable, try these tricks:

- Give yourself a reward. Have a latte or a nice healthy meal or a piece of dark chocolate after you complete your writing for the day. If you're counting calories, indulge in some other guilty pleasure.
- Have someone you trust regularly check on your progress. Writers' groups are particularly effective in this regard.
- Ask for help. Maybe the kids can make dinner; maybe your partner can do the laundry.
- For inspiration, go to a literary event at a bookstore, library, or online. Immerse yourself in the literary community any way you can.
- Read Dorothy Parker. She was a famous writer who hated writing.

If you are overwhelmed by writing, try these tricks:

- Break the writing into smaller, more manageable sections. Maybe you can only handle a page a day for now—maybe half a page early morning, half a page later.
- Write a chapter outline, and then commit yourself to completing each small section.
- Write the book out of order. Write the middle first, then the end, then the beginning. Scott Turow writes this way, and he does all right.
- Ask for help. Maybe you need a mentor or writing class to help you get—and keep—going.

FINDING YOUR WRITING RHYTHM

Conventional wisdom suggests that setting aside time early in the day every day is the best way to go, but this isn't always possible, and it may not suit your physiology or schedule. You're not off the hook, though; this just means you have to find the writing schedule and rhythm that works best for you.

If you have to scramble to get everyone ready for school and work in the mornings, perhaps you can write during your lunch hour or in the evenings. If you're a nurse or a firefighter and work long shifts, you may have to write more four days a week, to make up for not writing at all three days of the week. There is no requirement to write at the same time each day, as long as you schedule some writing time each and every day (or each and every day it is possible). As time goes by, you will find that certain circumstances work best for you. Pay attention to your body and brain. If you sit there staring at the computer in a total fog at 8 A.M., but find words flowing and fingers flying in the evening . . . well, duh—then don't try to write in the morning, no matter what we said at the beginning of this chapter.

Once you've figured out your best writing time, do everything you can to keep that time sacred. Be creative about where and when to get your writing done. (Speaking from bitter personal experience, Sam would not recommend writing on your laptop while floating in a pool. Bathtubs and playground swings are also bad ideas.)

As we said earlier, some authors can write at the dining-room table with family life swirling around them. Others can write on commuter trains and airplanes. We have personally seen Ridley Pearson hunched over his laptop writing on rock & roll tours—a time the rest of us Remainders think of as summer camp for so-called grownups who have temporarily forgotten how to read, let alone write.

But most writers do their best work in a serene, private, interruption-free environment. Many writers like to listen to music while they work, though some say that lyrics distract them and they prefer instrumental recordings. Others can write in front of the TV (though you may run the risk of having bits of *Law and Order* dialogue creep into your manuscript). Some like a room with a view; others like to work in small, closet-like spaces. In our household, Sam writes in an airy upstairs room facing the ocean, sometimes with a game on TV in the background. Kathi holes up in a cluttered office with red-lacquered walls and leopard-print pillows, blasting country-and-western classics (added benefit: non–country music fans will vacate the premises swiftly).

FIGURE OUT WHAT WORKS FOR YOU

You won't get far following someone else's rules or schedule. You have to pay attention to your own preferences and rhythms and do what works for you—but you also must be flexible. There will be times when you're nowhere near your Kitty Wells CD or your beloved 49ers (Wither Joe Montana? Wither Jerry Rice?). Guess what? You'll need to figure out how to roll into your Zone and write anyway. The only rule is this: your writing won't get done if you don't sit down and do it. So, how do you create circumstances that will help you produce? We're glad you asked.

- If you listen to music while you work, remember which track was playing when you last stopped writing. Engage your sense-memory by playing the same track again when you start. You can also do this with smells and visual cues.
- Turn off those digital alerts that let you know the instant an e-mail comes in.
- Shut down your e-mail altogether.
- Turn off your phone.
- Keep a notebook and pen or pencil with you at all times to jot down ideas that come when you're not at your usual workspace.
- Don't lose the notebook.
- Even if no one knows that you're writing a book, respect and honor the process. Treat your writing as you would any other important work. Would you go to the office in your pajamas and bunny slippers before brushing your teeth? Most people do better work if they're washed and groomed, have had a bit of breakfast, and remembered to get dressed—even if all that means is changing into a fresh pair of sweatpants.
- If you get stuck, take a walk. Four out of five scientists agree that physical activity will improve your circulation and dislodge blocked brain cells. The other scientist is on the sofa eating potato chips and watching reruns of *Law and Order*.
- Whatever you do, don't forget to get your magic rubber chicken out from under the divan, dress it in a scarlet sequined cape and Mouseketeer hat, pinch its nose, and wave it around your head three times. What? No one told you this is the secret ritual employed by every *New York Times* best-

selling author, particularly Anne Rice in her vampire period? We thought everybody knew . . .

WRITING ALONE VERSUS WRITING WITH OTHERS

Writing is a solitary process. You'll probably want to complete at least one draft of your work before showing it to anybody, and we advise reading the whole thing out loud (to yourself, the cat, or one trusted, supportive friend or family member). But don't show your work to just anyone at this stage, and please don't show it to everyone. You know that guy who thinks he's a terrific poet and sends you (along with many others on his list) long stream-of-consciousness e-mails every couple of days? Take it from us: you don't want to be that guy. You want to be the sweetly unassuming friend-of-a-friend who surprises everyone by getting a novel published. So keep it to yourself, or within a very small group, until you feel you've done the absolute best you can on your own.

WRITING GROUPS

No matter what you're writing, a time will come when you'll need to show your work to other people if you hope to get published. Writing groups can be a great midlevel forum, providing a valuable service for new writers—as long as you find the right group. Though it can be interesting and educational to join a group in which members write in different genres, you might get more out of a group that includes people who write in a similar genre to yours. Kathi once spent a very long evening as the only comic-fiction writer in a room full of authors of heart-wrenching memoirs, and ended up feeling like a callous jerk. Try to find people at approximately the same skill level, something that is hard to quantify and even harder to accomplish. Despite the matchmaking-disaster potential, it's worth giving writers' groups a try.

If you don't like any of the groups that exist in your community, you can start one of your own. As the leader, you'll be able to define the rules and pick and choose the members. If you have trouble finding other writers in your area, you can also create or join a virtual writing community online.

All writers' groups are different, and since *you* are starting the writers' group, *you* get to make up the rules. Is that cool or what? As the initiator, it will be up to you to set the tone and provide some guidelines. Here are some tricks that have worked for us and other writers' groups we know.

Finding Your Fellow Writers and Starting Your Group

Find members by asking your local bookseller or librarian or advertising online. It may take a while to gather exactly the right mix of people, but it's worth putting some effort (and patience) into this part of the process. All members should be within shouting distance of the same level of writing skill. This doesn't mean you all have to be working in the same genre—a variety of writing styles and themes can make for an interesting group.

Figure out how often it's practical to meet, then require that members make a commitment to attend all meetings. More writers' groups fall apart due to a casual attitude about attendance than any other reason. In this sense, writers' groups are no different than bowling leagues, softball teams, and poker games.

Try to meet in person, rather than online, if you possibly can—and have those whose work is being discussed read aloud. Reading aloud to others is the surest way to catch all sorts of little things in your own writing, like redundancies, awkward phrasing, and redundancies.

Who Reads What and When?

Decide how many pieces, and pages, will be read and discussed at each meeting. In a larger group you might want to take turns, with no more than three or four members' work being discussed at any one meeting. Distribute pages among group members at least a day or two before each meeting, so everyone has time to read and think about the material ahead of time.

Giving Helpful Feedback

Establish a positive tone. Even if a piece of writing needs a lot of work, find something good to say. Critique one another's work in a supportive and constructive manner, but do critique; it doesn't help the other writers if you see problems but are afraid to mention them. Be as specific as you can. "This doesn't work for me" is not as effective as "I think if you cut the first paragraph and started here, you'd have a more engaging beginning." The same rule applies to praise. Be very specific about what you like, and why. "You have a great sense of how to use dialogue—I can really tell one character from another" is more useful than, "Wow—you're a good writer!"

Always write your suggestions down on your copy of the pages, and return them to the author. If you are working digitally, do the equivalent—make sure that the author has a record of your thoughts.

Remember that the reason you are all in this group is to help each other improve. Watch for patterns and themes in the feedback that you receive. If three out of four people think you should lose the three-page description of a cornfield, well, they just might have a point. If three out of four readers strongly think you have a gift for young adult fiction, you might want to be open to that idea, even if you have always been convinced it is your destiny to write the defining, dark postmodern novel about adult angst and win the National Book Award. Maybe the postmodern novel is your *second* book. Develop your strengths and work on your weaknesses, and you are guaranteed to become a better writer. If four out of five dentists prefer Blatz beer, then maybe you should consider switching to Blatz.

You can also instigate a more casual form of writers' group by choosing one or two writer-friends and getting together in a café or at someone's home to write, rather than discuss, your respective work. You'll have some company, but there's no pressure to read anything out loud or submit to a critique. You'll have someone to share a pastry with and put on fresh sweatpants for. And with another writer or two in close proximity, you'll be less tempted to talk on the phone or check your e-mail. Let peer pressure work for you.

ATTEND A WRITERS' CONFERENCE

Writers' conferences can help you improve your writing and hone your message, and also offer opportunities to meet agents, editors, and other writers. Some conferences focus more on literary craft (these are sometimes juried—meaning you have to submit a sample of your writing and be accepted in order to attend); others focus more on sales and marketing; many cover both, and most welcome anyone willing to show up and pay the tuition. Do your research and choose a conference that best meets your needs and budget.

We recommend talking to others who have attended a particular conference before plunking down a lot of cash. You can also ask about scholarships, and there are often opportunities to volunteer your time in exchange for access to a conference.

Whether or not you end up making a connection that leads to publication, attending a writers' conference will allow you several days to concentrate on nothing but yourself and your writing (not to mention getting a welcome break from your job, husband, kids, and dog)—a true luxury. Chances are you'll learn a lot, too.

One online resource for finding the right conference for you is Writers' Conferences and Centers (WC&C) at *www.writersconf .org*.

GET CAUGHT READING

We can't think of any writer we know who didn't start out as an avid reader. Reading is what makes many of us decide to be writers; reading fuels our imaginations, and even helps us learn how grammar and syntax work. So read. Read as much as you can, all the time.

Except . . .

Some writers find that when they are deep in a project, it throws them off to read other people's writing. This seems to apply mostly to fiction and has to do with not allowing another voice to interfere with your own, and it's a viable and respectable position. But if you find yourself unaffected by others' writing styles (for example, if you're the type who can write while *Law and Order* is on and *not* find lines from the script creeping into your manuscript) then by all means read. Read a lot, read anything you want, read for fun. But don't read when you're supposed to be writing. And even if reading in your own genre distracts you or causes you to have difficulty writing, you don't have to stop reading altogether. Just read other good stuff and call it "research."

THE AUTHOR ENABLER'S CARE PACKAGE FOR WEARY AUTHORS

No matter how talented, disciplined, or even lucky you are, there will be days when you end up staring at a blank page or screen in utter despair. Even if you take every bit of advice in this book, we can't promise automatic bestselling success, or even 100 percent productive writing sessions. We'd like to offer a few comfort strategies for those *Mama said there'd be days like this* moments.

Take a comfort food break: It can really help soothe jangled nerves to eat something you love. (If someone you love prepares your treat from scratch, using a tried-and-true family recipe, all the better.) Here's one of Kathi's secret weapons: Grandma Clara's famous matzo ball soup. It's warm, soothing, and tasty—and turning off your brain for the time it takes to chop all those vegetables might even rejuvenate your creative juices. If you're not a matzo-ball lover then mashed potatoes, macaroni and cheese, or a quart of triple-fudge ice cream might work just as well. You'll have to come up with your own recipes for those.

The Soup
Serves eight with leftovers

One whole chicken
Enough water to cover chicken (see below)
Salt and pepper to taste
2 onions, chopped
1 pinch of sugar
6 carrots, chopped
1 parsnip, chopped
1 to 2 leeks, chopped
2 cloves garlic, chopped
6 stalks celery
A generous handful of parsley
1 tablespoon dill

1. Cover the chicken with water. Add salt, pepper, onions, and sugar.
2. Add carrots, parsnip, leeks, garlic, celery, and parsley to the mix.
3. Bring to a boil and simmer one and a half hours.
4. When chicken is falling off the bone, remove from the stove and strain the liquid into another pot. Add as much of the boiled chicken and other ingredients as you'd like; the rest of the veggie mush can go into the compost with the chicken bones.

Keep warm on the stove until your matzo balls are ready.

The Matzo Balls
This recipe makes approximately 16 matzo balls

4 teaspoons vegetable oil (if you don't keep kosher, use melted butter—you won't be sorry!)
4 large eggs, slightly beaten
1 cup matzo meal
3 tablespoons parsley, chopped
3 cloves garlic, chopped
Salt to taste
4 tablespoons of the soup

1. Mix together vegetable oil (or melted butter), eggs, matzo meal, a parsley, garlic, and salt.
2. Add the soup. Stir until loosely blended.
3. Cover the mixture and refrigerate for at least fifteen minutes—longer is fine.
4. Bring a large pot of water to a brisk boil.
5. While you are waiting for water to boil, roll matzo mix into balls approximately 1 inch in diameter.
6. Reduce flame and drop balls into the water.
7. Cover the pot and cook forty minutes.
8. Scoop matzo balls out and add them to the soup. Enjoy!

OTHER TRICKS FOR KEEPING IT FRESH

Take a musical break: Walk away from your writing for a few minutes to play, sing, or listen to a little music. Do you own a guitar, a violin, a clarinet, a zither, or a kazoo? Whatever your instrument, take it out of the case, buy an inexpensive stand (perhaps you can design your own kazoo stand), and keep it near your writing space. Play it once in a while. You can also indulge in one-minute "harmonica moments" and it just so happens that we know of a book to use to help you learn how to do this: *How to Play the Harmonica: and Other*

Life Lessons by Sam Barry. We would love this book even if one of us wasn't the author.

Take a movie break: There are so many wonderful, entertaining, and inspiring movies out there! The best thing about a movie break is that you can watch while playing the harmonica *or* eating soup. We don't recommend both at once. Dropping your harmonica into the soup is only one of the potential pitfalls. Here is a list of some favorites that are about—or feature scenes about—books, bookstores, and/or authors:

- *Stranger than Fiction* (both the author-care and IRS stuff are far-fetched—in real life, your publisher doesn't send Queen Latifah to help you finish your manuscript—but the story is fun)
- *Crossing Delancey* (the Amy Irving character works in a bookstore)
- *Bridget Jones' Diary* (has a funny scene involving Salman Rushdie)
- *You've Got Mail* (small indie bookstore is forced to close; some wonderful pretentious-author moments)
- *Borat* (includes a scene where they kidnap Pamela Anderson from her book-signing)
- *The Shining* (a writer slips into insanity in an isolated old hotel)
- *Chasing Amy* (all about comic book writers)
- *The 40-Year-Old Virgin* (Seth Rogen's character is writing a novel)
- *Harry Potter and the Chamber of Secrets* (exposes the silly, ego-driven behavior of some authors with the Gilderoy Lockhart character)

It doesn't have to be a movie. There's a great episode of the TV show *Stella* (available on DVD) all about the publishing industry. The episode is called "Novel." And in the television series *Mad Men* the characters spend a good deal of their work time trying to come up with hooks for their advertising campaigns.

Do something nice for someone else: a big thing (opening a homeless shelter or an urban tutoring center) or a little thing (washing someone else's dishes or taking the neighbor's dog for a walk)—it doesn't really matter. You'll be helping out, and you'll end up feeling better about yourself.

Get some fresh air and exercise: Perhaps the most tried-and-true method for restoring the creative spirit is something you learned to do before you ever started reading or writing. Take a walk. See a little patch of the outside world. Walk to the store, to a café, to the library, to a museum. You'll feel those endorphins kick in; they're good for writing and good for your waistline, too, especially after consuming seven or eight matzo balls. Don't forget to bring a notebook and pencil with you, just in case.

Whatever your strategies may be, it's crucial to give yourself a break now and then. You'll end up doing better work in the long run, we promise.

BOTTOM LINE

Your writing is more important to you than it is to anyone else. Honor the process, treat yourself and your work with respect, and take care of yourself, your sweatpants, and your creative process by making time and space to work. But—please, for Pete's sake—don't start acting self-important or copping an attitude. It's obnoxious and it won't get you any closer to your goals. The only thing that will help you get that book finished is one very simple thing: apply butt to chair, and write.

CHAPTER FOUR

YOUR MANUSCRIPT: THE BASIC RULES OF ATTRACTION

This chapter contains some simple rules that will make your manuscript more appealing and readable. You'll also be encouraged by a list of authors who had trouble getting their books published at first, then went on to dramatic success.

An agent or an acquiring editor must read and evaluate manuscript after manuscript, looking for the gems that they believe they can sell. Because they are pros, they recognize their views as subjective—that what they like is not the only measure of what is good or worthy, and that their personal likes and dislikes are not shared by everyone. In other words, no individual is going to appreciate every book, however good or bad the writing.

On the other hand, a successful agent must have a pretty sharp eye—that's why they are in the business—and agents will be more enthusiastic and do a better job selling and supporting quality work that suits each agency's particular skills and contacts. Literary agents have specialties. If you've written a good manuscript that doesn't play to a particular agent's taste, there are agents out there whose talents will be more appropriate. An agent who turns you down may even offer the name of another agent who specializes in representing your kind of book.

PUT YOURSELF IN THE AGENT'S SHOES

Let's say you are a successful literary agent and have just returned from the Maui Writers Conference where you were "working hard" sitting on panels (the beach) and making connections (drinking mai tais). You sit down to catch up on a backlog of work, which includes looking at several manuscripts on your desk. One is from a successful writer you already represent. Another is from a published writer you met at the conference who is between agents. You expressed interest in seeing the proposal for her next book. A couple of others are from people who sent you query letters per the guidelines on your website. You were interested enough to request the manuscripts, and here they are. And another pile consists of manuscripts that were sent to you unsolicited.

You check your voice mail, where you encounter a number of important and less important messages, ranging from editors at publishing houses getting back to you to your elderly mother calling to see if you will be visiting soon. Your e-mail inbox is full and there is a pile of snail mail on your desk.

Feeling overwhelmed, you settle into your favorite reading chair, pen and notepad in hand, and prepare to read the manuscripts. First you look at the submission from the author who is already in your stable. This person is a talented journalist who has one *New York Times* bestseller under his belt. However, his last two books have had disappointing sales. This new book is about the growing influence of Latino culture in America's public education system. The book summary is too general and the chapter outlines are a little perfunctory, but that can all be worked out. You already represent this author, so your perspective is that of partner. You look at the sample chapter and are quickly drawn into the narrative, which is no surprise, because this guy can write.

But you are worried. Why is this material best presented as a book, rather than a piece on public radio, or a magazine article? Why will a publisher plunk down a big chunk of cash up front for this proposal, when the public can get the same information elsewhere and the author has a declining sales track (meaning each successive title has sold less than the bestseller that got him all this attention)? You make a note to call him—an e-mail won't do.

Next you turn your attention to the author you met in Maui. She is a talented writer whose work straddles genres, landing somewhere between literary fiction and thriller. This can be a problem for publishers, who want their customers to know where to locate a book in bookstores. Her last book garnered critical acclaim and sold well, and you think she is a star on the rise. But then you aren't the only one who thinks this, which makes you wonder why she is shopping for a new agent. You worry that there may be some problem and make a note to do some quiet checking around, but in the meantime you are excited to look at her manuscript.

The beginning is superb, telling the tale of a woman driving up the coast in Northern California pursued by mysterious men in a van, and an hour goes by without your even noticing. But then the story begins to bog down in a second subplot about an eight-year-old runaway with a lame puppy. This second part of the book involves a lot of beautiful but aimless atmospheric writing and doesn't appear to have anything to do with the woman pursued by mysterious men. You wish you had a closer relationship with the author—you would tell her to make this subplot tie in more clearly with the primary story or cut it altogether. You wonder, also, if this is part of the unknown problem—that the author is not happy in the thriller genre, where sales tend to be larger, and is writing in a way that lends itself more to the literary work.

Tough Love from the Author Enablers

When sending query letters or manuscripts to agents or publishers, follow the submission guidelines or we'll come over and kick your butt (metaphorically speaking)! ‹ «

Next you turn to the two manuscripts from unpublished authors who are seeking representation. The first manuscript is a nonfiction work about space exploration and its effect on our belief in the afterlife. The idea and author sounded intriguing in the query letter, but it is immediately apparent that you will not be interested in representing this author. There is no short synopsis of the book, no author bio, no table of contents, no chapter summaries. You are immediately thrown into reading a manuscript that screams "academic." The first sentence is so long you can't remember where it began when you get to the end. But you could, maybe, overlook this if you were fascinated by what you are reading. The real issue for you is that the manuscript doesn't deliver on the promise of the initial query letter. It is not a tightly constructed argument from someone you immediately trust, nor is it a brilliant if tangential look inside a great mind. Rather it is just the boring thoughts of one more person, albeit a college professor, who has a lot to say on a subject with which he is clearly obsessed. But why should you care? Why should the world care? Why should a publisher risk a lot of money and many hours of employees' work on this professor's ideas? And ultimately the author should be thinking about the potential reader—someone who will be expected to shell out twenty dollars or more in a bookstore. There is nothing in the manuscript to convince you to go for it, and plenty to convince you otherwise. You make a note to decline.

The other solicited manuscript is by a mother of three who is just starting out on her career as a writer—not the likeliest scenario for bestsellerdom. But something about her query letter charmed you and you want to give it a shot. You are feeling grumpy because of your disappointment over the academic—you had really believed that that one might work—but you try to shake it off and settle into this new work.

You begin to relax as you read her cover letter, her brief, admittedly thin, yet charmingly honest bio. The one-paragraph synopsis is well constructed and to the point, as is the longer plot outline. She has even provided you with some comparison titles, and apparently has the ear of at least one well-known author who will provide a blurb.

But it is the writing that gets you. The first of the fifty pages your guidelines ask for draws you in instantly. Your office disappears as you go deep into this author's world. You want to represent her. You will send the e-mail immediately, along with a few suggestions. You are already thinking of the right editor at the right house.

Lastly, you look through the manuscripts that were sent to you unsolicited. If they have a return envelope with postage, you make a note to your assistant to send them back with the usual form letter that directs the author to read and follow your submission guidelines. Those that have no return envelope you place unceremoniously in the recycling bin. Why should you have to spend your hard-earned money returning them?

DON'T TAKE REJECTION PERSONALLY

Prospective bestselling writer, are you getting the idea? What to you is a cherished work of art or impassioned cause is part of someone else's workday. This imagined scenario is not intended to discourage you, but rather to get you out of yourself and into the shoes of those whom you must successfully engage—and who, in turn, must sell your work to others.

When you do get that manuscript returned in your self-addressed stamped envelope (SASE) with a form-letter rejection from either an agent or a publisher, you get to indulge in exactly twenty-four hours of feeling sorry for yourself, and then you have to get over it. Think about ways you can improve your manuscript or proposal, and do them. It's no fun to get rejected, but it happens to everyone and you can't let it keep you from working on your writing career.

AN EXAMPLE OF AN EFFECTIVE QUERY LETTER

Here's an especially good query letter, written (and generously shared with us) by our friend, author and writing coach Leslie Levine:

Dear _____ :

Do you save the wishbone? Do you pause before you blow out the candles? Does wishing make it so?

In *Wish It, Dream It, Do It: Turning What You Want into What Is Yours,* I will clearly, creatively, and gently show readers how to combine their dreams and wishes with practical strategies intended to help them achieve what they really want from life.

The person who follows her bliss doesn't simply gaze at the stars or daydream about becoming a millionaire. This dream catcher *does* something about what's missing in her life. And although she holds on to her dream like a hat on a cold and blustery day, she also engages in and embraces the hard, hard work that wishes and dreams require but rarely disclose. In other words, she will wish it, dream it, and, finally, do it.

In all 52 chapters—one for each week in the year—I will prescribe a three-part strategy that will help readers combine their inner resources with external sources of support, such as mentors, workshops, books, and friends and family. Each chapter will instruct readers to (1) ask, (2) experiment, and (3) affirm. For example, in the chapter "Listen to Your Quiet," I will provide questions such as "What have I not been hearing?" and "Am I giving my dreams a voice that's loud enough to hear?" Also, I will encourage readers to experiment with the what ifs, so that they can get a sense of what might happen if, indeed, they try on their dreams. In other words, I will show readers how to test themselves without worrying about failing or being judged. Each chapter will close with an affirmation—a show of support and a few words intended to coax readers toward taking the next step. Ultimately, readers will learn how to create and then live by their own affirmations.

I have thought about *Wish It, Dream It, Do It* ever since I began writing the manuscript for my second book, *Ice Cream for Breakfast: If You Follow All the Rules, You Miss Half the Fun* (Contemporary Books). Soon after I signed the contract I picked up the Wish It, Dream It, Do It affirmation in a gift shop. To this day it serves as a constant and rich source of inspiration. My dreams don't always come true, but I am a firm believer in the power of the tenacious human spirit. And I am convinced that people can pursue and often achieve their dreams if they can access the tools and strategies that very often move them from "wishing" to "doing."

My articles on topics ranging from home remodeling to parenting have appeared in *Woman's Day Remodeling Ideas, Better Home and Gardens Remodeling Ideas,* and *The New York Times.* My first book, *Will This Place Ever Feel Like Home? Simple Advice for Settling In After Your Move,* was published by Dearborn. I am frequently quoted on relocation issues and have been featured in the *Wall Street Journal, Los Angeles Times, Washington Post, Chicago*

Tribune, Parenting magazine, and other publications. Also, I have been a featured guest on the Today Show, CBS This Morning, Fox News, and WMAR-TV, the ABC affiliate in Baltimore. I have also been a radio guest on several stations across the country. Subsequent to the publication of *Will This Place Ever Feel Like Home?* I served as the national spokesperson for ERA Real Estate. In addition, I speak on a variety of topics including change, relocation, pursuing dreams, and breaking the rules.

Contemporary Books recently bought the rights to *Will This Place Ever Feel Like Home?* The initial print run for *Ice Cream for Breakfast* was 20,000. Contemporary Books also has right of first refusal for *Wish It, Dream It, Do It.*

While I am sending this query to a few other agents, Danielle Egan-Miller, my editor at Contemporary, specifically recommended that I contact you. In addition to providing a proposal, I would be happy to send you a copy of *Will This Place Ever Feel Like Home?* and/or a set of galleys for *Ice Cream for Breakfast.*

Thank you for your time and consideration. I can be reached at _____ or via e-mail at _____. I look forward to your response.

Best,
Leslie Levine

True Stories of Repeated Rejection Followed by Great Success:

STEPHEN KING

"When I was sixteen, I pounded a spike into my bedroom wall and started spiking rejection slips (I'd write the name of the rejected story on each pink slip). The spike tore out of the wall four years later. I was home on semester break from college when it went. I counted, and there were over 150 rejection slips on it (which didn't count the slips that came to my college dorm). After that I just piled them up. I sold my first story about eight months later." Stephen, the authors would like to note, went on to rock-and-roll stardom as the rhythm guitarist for the Rock Bottom Remainders and has had some success as an author, too.

MEG WAITE CLAYTON:

"My first novel, *The Language of Light*, was rejected by pretty much every publisher in the country, sat in a drawer for years, then was revived by the praise of a very kind Bharati Mukherjee when I pulled it out of the drawer and brought it to Squaw Valley Community of Writers. I submitted it to the Bellwether Prize, for which it was chosen as a finalist (but did not win). My agent asked if she could submit it and sold it to the first editor she sent it to. Similarly, *The Wednesday Sisters* was rejected by ten publishers when it was represented by one agent, only to receive multiple offers after I stripped the book back to what it had been when I signed with the first agent, found a new agent, and revised in a way that made sense to me."

CATHERINE BRADY

Author of *The Mechanics of Falling and Other Stories* and (by the way) winner of the Flannery O'Connor Award for short fiction: "For my first book of stories, I had a manuscript that I kept dithering with and retooling, but couldn't sell. It was even a runner-up in a few contests, but no dice. I am a slow learner, and one day it dawned on me that the book needed to be a REAL collection—to contain stories that really worked together. (Prior to this, I'd just been tossing in whatever I had available.) I threw out several stories and wrote some new ones so that the book would have a strong focus on Irish American immigrant women, and many of the stories in this version were related. Writers often talk about getting rejected in one place and sending a book elsewhere, but at least in my case and to my huge surprise, a publisher that had rejected a novel I'd sent the year before decided to accept this book for publication. It was probably foolhardy for me even to have sent it to the same publisher, but it worked. You just can't second guess or try to finesse this trying, unpredictable process."

JOE QUIRK

"I am the Rejection King! I own 375 rejection letters. When I sent the first chapter of my first novel *The Ultimate Rush* to a publisher who will remain unnamed, I received my 371st form rejection, and scribbled across the bottom were the words, 'Give it a rest, pal.' A few months later, Molly Friedrich sold the book to William Morrow on the strength of that first chapter. It made the *Boston Globe* bestseller list, St. Martin's bought the paperback rights for a quarter million, and Warner Brothers bought and then renewed the film option. Author Steve Kelly, writing for the *Richmond Review*, called it 'One of the best opening sequences of any novel I have read.'"

ANDREW SEAN GREER

Author of *The Confessions of Max Tivoli* and *Story of a Marriage:* "My own story is that I read somewhere, back in my early twenties, that you had to amass two hundred rejection letters before you ever published anything. It was the kind of information that you hold on to tightly as an aspiring author, but which has really no helpful meaning to it. Of course my thought was: 'Well let's make that go as quickly as possible!' So I wrote stories quickly, sent them out many at a time to dozens of magazines, and started a binder of rejection notes. I remember the *Atlantic* being particularly wonderful, from C. Michael Curtis. I even recall one from *Esquire* that was hand-written—it started to become important if they were hand-written, or completely standard. I think the meanest ones were bitter boilerplate: 'Most of the stories we reject have either A. a mother in bright red lipstick; B. a miscarriage; C. a dream sequence; or D. all of the above' and they would circle which one mine had (lipstick). And then one day I came home to my tiny apartment in Missoula, Montana to hear a voice on my answering machine: 'Andrew, this is Richard Ford and I'm editing *Ploughshares* and loved your story, wondered if you would let us use it for the next edition. . . .' How many rejection letters had I amassed over those two years? Almost exactly two hundred. No kidding. What scientific law can we take from this experience? Absolutely nothing. There's only one rule: persevere. One rejection or two hundred, a good story will always be published."

SUZANNE KAMATA

Author of *Losing Kei:* "I had high hopes for my first literary novel, a coming-of-age story about a mermaid-obsessed girl in Michigan who falls in love with a Gypsy. An early version was a finalist for an award for novels in progress, and I published a chapter as a short story in a literary magazine. I even signed with a literary agent. Unfortunately, I was so grateful to snag any agent at all, that I didn't check her credentials. She ultimately referred me to a book doctor that, as it turned out, was under investigation for fraud. Fool that I was, I shelled out a thousand dollars. After I cut ties with the agent, I submitted my novel a few more times to small presses and big agents, got some useful feedback, then set the novel aside for awhile to work on something else. I wrote stories, essays, another novel (this one about an all girl rock band), publishing in literary journals and e-zines from time to time. Then, I wrote another novel, *Losing Kei*. This one was set in Japan, and concerned an expat mother trying to regain custody of her bicultural son. Shortly after a chapter appeared in a literary magazine, I received an e-mail from an agent. She wound up representing me and sold my novel to Leapfrog Press."

LESLIE LEVINE

"When my first book, *Will This Place Ever Feel Like Home? Simple Advice for Settling In After You Move* was first being shopped around (by agent number one) it was rejected by, among others, Contemporary Books. Some years later, after it went out of print at Dearborn another company wanted to pick it up. Which company? Contemporary, of course. So somewhere in the paper trail that holds up my house there are two very different letters from the same publishing company: one is a little more hopeful than the other, but the two of them together offer a slightly different interpretation of a commonly heard bit of wisdom: when one door closes, another from the very same house (pardon the pun) may open a few years later . . ."

AMY TAN

Author of *Saving Fish from Drowning:* "Early on, when I was just starting to write the stories that would become part of *The Joy Luck Club*, my brand new and very optimistic agent sent a story of mine to the *Atlantic* and *New Yorker*, which were the two great literary venues for short stories at that time. I recently found the rejection letter, dated September 1, 1987, from Mike Curtis, the fiction editor of the *Atlantic*. He says, 'The Amy Tan is beautifully written, and I hope you'll send us more of her work. This story, however, tries to cover much ground, and seems to us a bit too thin. Maybe the next one.'

"I was excited to get more than a standard rejection letter and from the top editor himself. But I was also struck at the time that my story was referred to as '*The* Amy Tan.' I had become an entity. The story was actually titled, 'Waiting Between the Trees.' And I have to say now that I agree with him—as a short story, it does not work. It does not have a short story shape. As a chapter in a book, it works better, but is still, as Mike says, 'thin' as a story. It is more about the internal voice of this woman who feels she is invisible to her daughter. The story was later included in *The Joy Luck Club* and a year later, Mike did take a story called 'Two Kinds,' which also became part of the book. And to add to the 180 degree irony, a year after I was published, I was one of three judges who had to read and select three writers for a fellow-ship. Mike Curtis was one of the other judges and our tastes were very similar.

"Until I was published, that was the best rejection letter I had ever received. Like Stephen King, when I started to write fiction, I put up a bulletin board, which I intended to cover with rejection letters. That would prove I had been seri-ous enough with my writing to send out what I considered a finished piece and to then get going on a new story. I even thought I might create a decoupage of those letters and use that as wallpaper. I received some rejection slips with the stan-dard lines: 'Thank for sending us your story. We are sorry that we did not like it enough to include it in our magazine.' One was on a 1" x 8" strip—obviously cut from a page with these two lines repeated top to bottom. That original page had seen plenty of time in the copier, had been cut into thousands of strips, and sent to thousands of unhappy writers. It was a big deal to get a rejection letter with a handwritten note. I had one from the *New Yorker* that was encouraging in her rejection. It said: 'Try us again,' A number of years later, I received a letter from the *New Yorker* asking me if I had anything they could publish. Now that was stunning.

"I do think that editors have particular tastes. The gist of some letters said: 'Not for me,' meaning, 'this might appeal to some other editor, but it's not for me.' That was brought home to me when I received two rejections for *The Joy Luck Club* at around the same time. One said, in effect, that he liked the universal emotions of story but thought the voice was too ethnic and contrived. The other said that he liked the universal qualities of the voice, but thought the story was too ethnic and contrived.

"I later met one of those editors in an inadvertent way. I had gone to a writers' conference in Old Chatham with my editor to meet up with one of her writers. At one point, we found ourselves at the back of a room where an editor of a very literary house was standing before a fireplace, giving a fireside chat on what an editor looks for. He made a point about literary tastes by saying, 'I was one of the editors who received a manuscript of *The Joy Luck Club*. And I read it and I rejected it, because it was not for me.' It seemed that every-one in that room knew I was there, except the editor. He went on: 'And even though that book appealed to many people and went on to do very well, I would still say that book is not one I would publish.' At this point, the whole room was buzzing and people had turned around to see how I was reacting to this. The editor then saw me, turned around, grabbed a poker iron and said, 'Should I plunge this through me now or in the privacy of my room?' I was laughing, and I said that I agreed with what he said, that there are books that appeal to us for various reasons, and others that don't, and an editor should never be swayed by a larger public opinion."

WENDY NELSON TOKUNAGA

Author of the novels *Midori by Moonlight* and *Love in Translation*: "A book I like to recommend to writers for inspiration is *The Resilient Writer: Tales of Rejection and Triumph from 23 Top Authors* by Catherine Wald. The book is made up of in-depth interviews with writers such as Janet Fitch, Wally Lamb, Elinor Lipman, Bret Easton Ellis, and Amy Tan, who tell their stories of how they withstood the pain and frustration of rejection and criticism and continued to persevere on the often rocky road to publication. These writers offer valuable insights into both the creative process and the intricacies of the publishing world, as well as some much needed comfort that certainly helped me as I tried to keep my confidence up as I weathered my own rejections."

BOTTOM LINE

When communicating with agents and publishers, it's crucial to be courteous and professional and to follow their submission guidelines. Try to understand the process from the other person's point of view. As you can see, the work of many—if not most—writers gets rejected at times. You need to approach the goal of getting published with the endurance and determination of a long-distance runner.

CHAPTER FIVE

FINDING AN AGENT

Agents really are out there looking for good writers with fresh ideas. Yes, it can be hard to get their attention, but for most authors signing with an agent is the way to go, and we know a few top-secret tricks to help you in your agent search. Here's how to research and identify the live ones, how to get their attention, and how to avoid becoming a nuisance.

Before we discuss the agent search we want to make sure we're clear on something—we think most authors should be represented by an agent, but we are not saying you *have* to get one. There are certain genres (such as romance and science fiction) and certain publishers (such as academic and smaller presses) where editors are more likely to consider unsolicited submissions.

WHY YOU MAY NEED AN AGENT

A good literary agent will not only sell your book to a publisher, but will also be your champion and advocate throughout the whole publishing process. Some publishers won't even look at unsolicited manuscripts that are not represented by an agent. So what do these agents do? Glad you asked.

CONTRACT NEGOTIATIONS

If you do try to sell your book without representation, you'll be left alone to deal with your publisher and an almost indecipherable contract should your book be purchased. Reading and negotiating contracts is one of the ways in which agents earn their 15 percent commission, and we think it is worth it to have one in your corner.

The Author Enablers' Guide to the Right Writing Rights

What is it that your agent actually sells when your manuscript is acquired by a publisher? It boils down to the right to publish, distribute, and sell your original work. Most often, in a book-publishing deal the agent negotiates the grant of "primary rights"—hardcover, paperback, mass market, e-book, direct mail, and language(s)—but may retain some subsidiary rights to sell on your behalf. Subsidiary rights might be sold directly or through a subagent to book clubs, foreign publishers, movie or television producers, and so on. Keep in mind that any money a publisher pays you is an advance against future earnings.

Some other specialized, subsidiary (or secondary) rights include: animation, anthology, audio, book club, digest, dramatic, electronic/new technology, entertainment, foreign translation, large print, merchandising (commercial tie-in), motion picture, performance, periodical, (first-serial, like pre-publication excerpts or second serial), radio, television, theater, and videocassette/audiocassette/DVD. Phew!

Now, what if you want to use someone else's original work in your book? Though it may be tempting (and easy, now that we have the Internet), it's not okay to do this without permission, and permission often has to be paid for. (Most publishers have permissions departments and are open to direct queries.)

For example, if you want to use lyrics from a song written by someone else, you must get permission from whomever owns the rights to the property—and that entity is often not the performer, or even the composer, of the song. A little research on *www.bmi.com* and/or *www.ascap.com* (the two largest music-rights organizations) will usually provide the information you'll need. You'll have to find out who wrote the song, and who owns the copyright—then it is up to you, the author, to contact the copyright holders and arrange to pay whatever fee is required for usage. Your publisher will want to know that you have the legal right to use the material, so be sure to include copies of your agreement(s) with the copyright holder(s) when you submit your manuscript.

Using visual art requires a similar process. The first step is to locate the images you wish to obtain and figure out who can provide a copy. Sometimes it's a museum, sometimes a commercial image bank. Then you need to make a formal request for usage in your book. If you need help phrasing your letter, there's a good template in *The Chicago Manual of Style*. You may be asked to fill out an additional application, but you can get the ball rolling with a simple, businesslike letter. Keep in mind that reproducing color illustrations is expensive. Before you decide to include four-color art in your book, think through whether it is absolutely necessary. Additionally, it's not always the author's decision, but that of the publisher.

It's important to understand the difference between "copyright permissions" and "use permissions." The copyright for a work (a painting, a sculpture, a drawing) is usually not held by the owner of the physical work. For example, you might want to reproduce a painting found in the Museum of Modern Art in New York. At your request, the museum may provide a color transparency, or a high-resolution digital file, along with nonexclusive world rights to reproduce this image in your book, but all that the museum has granted is the USE of their reproduction; you must still obtain reproduction permission from the owner of the copyright, the estate of the artist. Both use and copyright permissions are required before a publisher can comfortably go forward with a book that includes a copyrighted image.

With both music and visual art, some older works will fall into the public domain category. This means that copyright no longer applies to the work. Laws vary from country to country, but the safest rule of thumb is that the work slips into the public domain seventy years after the author's or artist's death. However, this is not a hard and fast rule—many estates still hold on to the rights after the author has died. Even if a work is in the public domain, you may still need to get a "use" permission. For example, certain museums and collections will require a permission application for the use of their reproduction, and they will ask that you meet certain conditions, even if the work itself is in the public domain.

If this is confusing, think of it this way: you probably wouldn't want anyone using your writing, music, or artwork without your permission, especially if the usage resulted in profit that wasn't shared with you. So do your homework, and start acquiring the rights you need well in advance of your manuscript deadline. At the very least, it's good Karma.

ARE YOU READY? LET THE SEARCH BEGIN!

Before you begin your agent search, your manuscript or proposal should be fully conceived and in good shape. You may also want to establish some credibility as a writer by having shorter pieces published in journals or periodicals, if at all possible.

"Okay, big-shot Author Enablers," you might say. "*You* have an agent (a lovely woman named Deb Warren who sold this book to Adams Media) but how do I get one?"

There are several tried-and-true methods for acquiring agents' contact information. Finding an agent to represent you involves a mix of ingredients that includes some focused effort and good timing, as well as the aforementioned sticktoitiveness.

We're going to start by giving you the same advice you'd get before a job interview: know the people you are pursuing. It's a waste of everyone's time pitching an agent or agency with material that isn't a good fit. You want to find *the* agent who is right for you. Begin networking in the world of publishing and among other writers. As in a job search, it's helpful (but not a guarantee by any means) to be referred by a client, someone in the publishing industry, or a friend.

But first, a few words of warning. After a group reading by several authors who'd contributed to an anthology, the conversation turned to a discussion of the various authors' agents. One woman gushed about hers, and another—who was looking for someone to represent her new book—was intrigued.

"Your agent sounds great," she said innocently. "Will you tell me who she is and how to contact her?"

"Sure," said the more established author. "Can I date your boyfriend?" (Actually it was a different verb, but here at Author Enablers headquarters we frown on the public use of this verb. So date you.)

This is an extreme example, and we're not saying we approve of this behavior, but you might be surprised at how close-mouthed published authors can be about divulging their agents' names until/unless they've read your work and think it's (a) terrific and (b) a good fit for their agent. Despite the air of mystery, you must remember that there are many literary agents looking for good writers with fresh ideas. Yes, it can be hard to get their attention, and yes, there are hoops to jump through, but you can research and identify the "live ones" without having to rely on the luck of chance meetings or calling in favors with your writer friends.

"Great," you say. "You just told us a story about why not to do this, and anyhow, how do I meet the client of an agent, someone in the publishing industry, or the friend of an agent?" Okay, this might not work for everyone. Relying on personal contacts is only one approach to cracking the agent code. And if you don't have any contacts in the publishing business or know any writers, we're not suggesting you start handing out your manuscript to authors at bookstore readings or accosting agents on the streets of Manhattan. *You* want to be accosted by *them*.

So where do you find agents? We're glad you asked. There are several publications that provide listings of literary agencies. One of the best known is the *Literary Market Place*, an extensive listing of publishing professionals, a publication found in most libraries as well as online. In *LMP* you'll find agents listed along with their specialties and interests. Most agents also have websites that define their submission requirements. It's not in your best interest to ignore these requirements, as many agents have assistants who make the first cut according to adherence to these simple guidelines. There are other publications that can help in this quest, such as the publications produced by Writer's Digest and online newsletters like *Publishers Lunch*. Some books and online sites also offer agent listings—your librarian or local bookseller can lead you to the most up-to-date. Most important is making sure you have access to the most current information. Once you've identified some promising agencies, you can often check for guidelines and preferences on their websites.

If you can afford the time and tuition, writers' conferences and workshops are wonderful places to meet agents. For instance, the San Francisco Writers' Conference offers an event called "Speed Dating for Agents" that allows you access to several agents in the space of an hour. Other writer's conferences offer one-on-one meetings with agents, as well as many other benefits including an environment in which you can think about nothing but writing for a week or a weekend.

THE AUTHOR ENABLERS' TOP-SECRET AGENT-FINDING TRICK

Here is the Author Enablers' top-secret trick for identifying the best and most successful agents in your genre. Go to a bookstore or library and read the acknowledgment pages in books similar to yours. Most authors will thank their agents, and if you see certain names popping up over and over again, you'll know that these are the names of agents who successfully sell books in your genre.

NOW THAT YOU HAVE YOUR LIST OF AGENTS

Okay, you've figured out what your genre is, and found a list of reputable agents who represent books similar to yours. What's next?

FICTION WRITERS

If you are an unpublished writer and you have a completed work you want to sell, start by crafting your best query letter, and then follow it up with sample pages that will knock the socks off an agent. If you write genre fiction—a loose publishing term that generally refers to categories such as romance, horror (some say there's little difference), science fiction, fantasy, and thrillers— then you may want to join one of the appropriate organizations, such as Romance Writers of America, Sisters in Crime, Mystery Writers of America, or Science Fiction & Fantasy Writers of America, so you can network with other writers in your genre. Recommendations by previously published authors carry weight with agents. Also, why not join a writers' group? The support of a group and improvement to your craft can only help you in your quest to write the best possible book and find representation. You may even end up in a group with other writers who have been published before, know the ropes, and can help you make connections. If writing literary fiction, get noticed by submitting your writing to literary magazines and contests. Build up those credentials. If you attended a Master of Fine Arts (MFA) program for writing don't forget to note this in your resume and bio, and put those student and faculty contacts to use in any reasonable way you can. But don't be a pest.

NONFICTION WRITERS

Credentials are crucial for nonfiction authors—especially for business or self-help books. It is very difficult to sell a nonfiction proposal to a major house unless you are an expert on your subject and/or you have an established platform. Your platform might include some of the following elements:

- Media contacts in television, print, and radio
- A syndicated or regionally popular column
- A significant online presence (e-zine, website, blog, and so on)
- Published articles in a field that is directly related to the subject of your book
- An affiliation with a known and respected university or an eminent position among the clergy
- Twenty or more speaking engagements a year

Our point is, if you are a nonfiction writer, generally you need to bring something to the table besides your great proposal that will convince an agent that there's an audience out there for your work.

Regardless of your genre, remember to be courteous and respectful when you talk to agents. In fact, remember to be courteous and respectful when speaking to anyone—it is the right thing to do, and it will get you much further in life.

If an agent is disrespectful to you then you don't want to be represented by him or her. A good agent will return your e-mails or calls, keep you informed on the status of your submissions, and will send you your payments promptly. Most legitimate agents *do not* charge fees for consultations. Agents make money selling authors' work to publishers. If an agent wants to charge you money just to look at your writing, the Author Enablers think you should walk away. And if an agent turns out to be a jerk, crazy, lazy, or just plain stupid, then you don't want that agent to represent you.

Tough Love from the Author Enablers

Are you selling, or selling out? If it sounds like we are advising you to sell out your art—well, when it comes to your book, it's time to sell, if not sell out. After all, if you don't sell the book, very few people will get to read it—and isn't getting read the whole point? If you can't pitch the book in a clear, compelling, succinct way, then there's a good chance your agent won't be able to, either. *Remember: the inability to concisely summarize a book is often a sign that the concept is not well conceived.*
‹ «

QUERY LETTERS 101

A good query letter is brief and to the point. It should grab agents by the lapels and make them want to represent you. One page is fine, or two at most. You should summarize your book in a sentence or two, in a fashion similar to the "logline" of a Hollywood-style elevator pitch. For example:

- In this compelling debut novel, a depression-era Southern lawyer represents a black man in a rape trial; children learn deep, hard truths.
- In this charming picture book for beginning readers, a reindeer learns the value of his embarrassing bright red nose and finds his place in world.

- In this epic historical novel, God invents the world in six days and takes a vacation. Capers ensue.

In your query letter, start by letting the agency know why you contacted them. Were you referred by someone? Why is this agency the one for your book? Next, pitch your book: what is your novel or nonfiction proposal, and why is it a great book idea? If you have a story or anecdote that conveys your idea, use it now—don't save it for later. Be clever or charming, deep or exciting—strike a tone that is appropriate for you and your work, but do your best to grab the agent's attention.

Say why you are the person to write the book. If it's a novel, what is your writing background? What programs or conferences have you attended? Have you been published before, or won any awards? Who are your literary mentors and idols?

If your work is nonfiction, what are your credentials? Who is your audience? Do you have a platform? If your book is about the circus, it's more important to let them know that you ran away and joined the circus when you were ten years old than that you attended Stanford University (and to us, more interesting, but then we wish *we* had joined the circus). The point is to make clear why you are the person to write this book. But lying won't get you anywhere—don't pretend to be someone you aren't. What is called for is a good fit between the book you are proposing to write and yourself.

Finally, thank the agent for taking the time to read your materials, and remember to provide your contact information: phone number, address, and e-mail. Allow six weeks or so for a reply, and don't be a pest—nagging won't win you any friends.

There is no exact formula, and this entire process could take as long as a year, or even more. It's an important step to gain the representation of a literary agent, and there really aren't any magic shortcuts. Remember, you only need one agent, and it's worth putting in the time and energy to find the one that's right for you. In the process you will learn a lot about yourself, your writing, and your book. You won't just be someone who longs to be an author—you will be on your way.

To speed things along it is okay to send queries to more than one agency at a time unless you've promised someone an exclusive read. If you do make such a promise, limit it to a month or so. Have a clear deadline, after which it is agreed it is okay for you to send your work to other agencies.

CONGRATULATIONS! NOW GET BACK TO WORK

Perhaps you're in the shower, at the dentist's office, or even at work. Wherever you are, when *the* phone call comes—the one from the literary agent who has responded to your query letter, read your manuscript, and wants to represent you—you'll never forget the moment. Enjoy it, relish it, write about it in your journal, call your best friend, celebrate with a bottle of champagne and a great meal, and then get over it. You have a lot of important work ahead of you. Maybe your mother, your best friend, and even your writing group cronies think your manuscript is perfect, but your new agent is likely to recommend a rewrite. It's a good idea to listen to what the pros have to say and to choose your battles wisely.

More and more, agents are taking on some of the role of editors, and in a competitive marketplace, no one wants to pitch any book by a new author that isn't as near perfect as possible. This doesn't mean you won't have more work to do once your book is sold; it does mean that it's very likely you'll be asked to make some revisions before your agent is willing to take your book to market.

This is a crucial time in your publishing career, and also in what everyone involved hopes will be a long and fruitful association between two professionals.

"*The* phone call" will probably catch you by surprise when it comes. Still, it's your responsibility to be a pro. Here's the right way to handle the phone call:

Phone: Ring, ring!

You: Hello?

Agent: Shaquille Farquar? This is Ethel Bluestocking from the Bluestocking Literary Agency.

You: (*breathless, quickly turning down the volume on* Yo Gabba Gabba *and making the international sign for "I'm on the phone and it's important" to your highly evolved and understanding children*) Hello, Ms. Bluestocking. What can I do for you?

Agent: Well, for starters, you can let me represent you as an emerging new voice in contemporary fiction. I just read your pages and I adore your writing and a lot of your story line. I have a few suggestions for improvement, and hope that you can send me a revision with some minor changes. Assuming we can come to an agreement on a few matters, I'd like to be your agent.

You: (*overwhelmed by the "emerging new voice" business—and did she just say she wanted to represent you? But what did she mean by "a few matters"?*) Thank you so much. What sort of changes did you have in mind?

Ethel proceeds to tear your manuscript to shreds, but she does so with genteel politeness and exquisite manners. She asks for nothing less than a rewrite that basically eliminates your main character and follows a side plot instead—and goes on to tell you why she thinks these changes will make your book much more salable. You feel a lot of emotions at once—like the teacher just called on you, but you weren't paying attention and have no idea what the question is; angry; hurt, embarrassed; maybe even scared. You desperately want representation, but you don't want to make a huge mistake. You need a little time, and you decide to ask for it.

You: Uh, that's an interesting perspective. May I take just a little time to think this over?

Agent: Absolutely.

You hang up, still confused. You are afraid you may have already lost Ethel because you dared to ask for time to think. You also wonder if Ethel is right for you—after all, you are the author and you worked for years to get to this point. Who is she to offer such sweeping criticisms of the writing you took years—nay, a lifetime—to produce? On the other hand, you are suddenly closer than you have ever been to your goal of getting published, and someone in the publishing world has taken your writing seriously. You find yourself increasingly intrigued by Ethel's suggestions. You're not sure what you'll decide to do, but you do think it's worth giving the matter some serious thought. You start calling everyone in your writing group.

And here's the wrong way to handle that very same phone call:

Phone: Ring, ring!

You: Hello?

Agent: Shaquille Farquar? This is Ethel Bluestocking from the Bluestocking Literary Agency.

You: (*breathless, quickly turning off* Yo Gabba Gabba *and shaking a threatening fist at your children, who immediately start to fight with each other*) Hello, Ms. Bluestocking. What can I do for you? I said, "Shut up!" Didn't you hear me the first time?

Agent: Excuse me?

You: Oh, sorry. I wasn't talking to you. What can I do for you?

Agent: Well, for starters, you can let me represent you as an emerging new voice in contemporary fiction. I just read your pages and I adore your writing and a lot of your story line. I have a few suggestions for improvement, and hope that you can send me a revision with some minor changes. Assuming we can come to an agreement on a few matters, I'd like to be your agent.

You: Changes, huh? What kind of changes? Everyone I know who's read it thinks it's brilliant.

Ethel proceeds to tear your manuscript to shreds, etc.

You: Whoa, *excuse me?* I spent years working on that book. I don't think you're the agent for me. Thanks, but no thanks.

Agent: Would you like to take a little time to think this over?

You: I guess I can give it some thought. *How many times do I have to tell you guys to put a lid on it?*

Agent: Excuse me?

You: No! That's not yours!

Agent: Sorry?

You: Oh, uh, sorry, something going on here. Kids, you know. So where were we?

Agent: Perhaps we should talk at a better time.

You end the phone call and hang up, finding yourself increasingly pissed off by Ethel's suggestions, pushing away the annoying thought that she might have a point. As you sit alone, stewing about the call, you come to realize that Ethel is an idiot. No one, not even Ethel Bluestocking, tells you what to change in the next Great American Novel.

DON'T JUMP TO CONCLUSIONS

Here's the thing: Ethel might be right (she probably knows a lot more than you do about what sells, and even what constitutes good writing and a well-told story), but if you can't see yourself making the changes she suggests, you shouldn't sign with her agency. Still, it might be worth taking a little time to think things over. We think it is always a good idea to discuss important decisions with a trusted friend or two. If they haven't read your work, ask them to read it now in light of Ethel's suggestions. There is no reason to rush this decision. The important thing is to take Ethel's criticism seriously and to make the decision about whether or not to have her represent you in a businesslike manner. Try doing a little writing along the lines she suggests to see how it goes, instead of delivering an immediate, flat-out yes or no.

Tough Love from the Author Enablers

Be a pro. Writing for publication means you will experience some rejection, other people's opinions, and endless rewrites. If you're not up for this, it really is fine to stick to journaling.

Remember, finding the right agent can be a long and somewhat painful process. You are doing a brave thing putting yourself and your work out into the world, and those are growing pains you are feeling. ‹ ‹‹

In real publishing life, an agent is likely to ask for changes that are less dramatic, but there will almost always be a request for revisions. Our suggestion is that you be a good sport and give it a try. Don't sell yourself down the river, but don't dismiss out of hand a suggestion that might be creative and sound, either.

When you find a literary agent to represent you, chances are you'll be asked to sign a contract in blood. Just kidding. A signed contract isn't required, but may be more comfortable for both of you. Of course, it's easier to end the relationship if there is no contract.

Most author-agent agreements give the agent exclusive rights to represent your work worldwide in all media and in all formats, though some contracts are limited to a specific work or specific media. (For example, some authors have one agent for publisher negotiations and another for film rights.)

The term of the agreement can range from thirty days to the duration of the work's copyright. Agents are most interested in signing clients they think will be around (and salable) for many years to come, but as an author, you have a legitimate interest in not getting stuck with an agent who is unproductive. For you, the best deal is a thirty-day "at will" termination provision (meaning that either party may terminate the agreement with thirty days' written notice). Some contracts provide for a nonterminable six-month period followed by a thirty, sixty, or ninety-day termination clause. You can also ask for an "out" clause that will allow you to end the agreement if the agent has not made a sale within an agreed-upon time limit. But even if you sever ties with the agency, your agent is entitled to receive commissions for all deals made on your behalf during the term of the agreement.

Most agents charge 15 percent, plus an additional 5 to 10 percent for foreign rights, and many agents will charge their authors for title-related expenses such as copying and postage. Most agency agreements provide that the agent will receive all of the author's royalties and advances directly from the publisher, and pay the author after deducting the appropriate reimbursements and commission. Payments to the author should be made within ten days after being received by the agent. If that doesn't happen, you'll need to hire another kind of agent, if you catch our drift.

BOTTOM LINE

There are a lot of people who want to get published. Of course *we* know that you are special and your work is far superior to theirs (especially if you take all our advice), but the market is very competitive. Agents are in a position to pick and choose. Do everything to make sure they pick and choose *you*.

CHAPTER SIX

BEHIND CLOSED DOORS: WILL THEY BUY YOUR BOOK?

What happens at those mysterious meetings in which publishers decide what to publish and what not to publish? We'll take you behind the scenes to see for yourself.

OUR MADE-UP TRUE-LIFE ACCOUNT OF A PUBLISHING MEETING

"The End."

Whoa, it's really fun typing that, let's do it again: "The End."

Woo Hoo! This is a bigger thrill than the water-slide at Clown Town because, most often, when you type these words it means you've finished writing a book (unless you're a postmodernist).

As tremendous an accomplishment as that may be, you should know that finishing a book is just the beginning of your work as an author. There's the nail-biting agent search, of course, and the decisions about where and to whom to submit your manuscript. Some writers even have trouble figuring out when they're finished revising and ready to share their genius with the world. The fact is that once your book starts making the rounds of publishers it will never be wholly and completely yours again. If you're ready for that, take a look behind the scenes at a mysterious publishing phenomenon called the "Editorial Board meeting" (or "Pub Board," short for "Publisher's Advisory Board" meeting).

OUR MADE-UP TRUE-LIFE ACCOUNT OF A PUBLISHING MEETING

Here's how it works. Let's say you've written a fictional page-turner about murder and mayhem in a bird-watching club. You've done your research, sent out query letters, and found Ethel Bluestocking, a veteran literary agent eager to sell your novel, *When the Sparrow Cries Wolf,* to a publisher.

Ms. Bluestocking has written a charming cover letter and sent your manuscript to several editors in trade publishing. She probably started with editors she knows well, or those with whom she's had recent success. A good agent knows the landscape of editorial departments; a great agent knows a lot about the personal tastes of editors and the unique character of each list. A super-agent like Ethel Bluestocking knows that Barry Samuels, Senior Editor at Ballpoint Publishing (a division of Unimax Inc., the global media empire), is a die-hard bird-watching enthusiast with a penchant for murder mysteries.

Barry Samuels loves the idea of your book, but has some issues with character development and plot lines. He feels confident that with his expert editorial guidance, *When the Sparrow Cries Wolf* could be the fine book it is meant to be, and he writes a memo explaining why. He then adds your manuscript to the agenda of the next Editorial Board meeting, and distributes your bio, marketing ideas, plot synopsis, and a few sample chapters to the colleagues who regularly attend this meeting.

THE PLAYERS

Editorial board meetings are scheduled once every couple of weeks, and usually include some variation of the following cast of characters:

Publisher: Oversees all aspects of the imprint's business and has the final word on submissions.

Editorial Director (or Chief Editor): Oversees the editorial staff; the editorial director is often the person who runs the meeting.

Acquiring Editor: Sifts through proposals and determines which will be of greatest interest to the imprint, and ultimately, the reader. The editor is the person your agent shows your book proposal to; he may or may not want to have a conversation with you before presenting your proposal to the board. In addition to acquiring manuscripts, editors help their authors seek endorsements, get excerpts published, advocate for the authors in-house, and—oh yeah—edit their books, though at some publishing companies there is a second editor who does the actual editing.

Marketing Director: Oversees the development of materials designed to help the sales force get orders from retailers, including catalogue copy, cover design, in-store displays, advertising, online presence, giveaways and promotions, outreach to organizations, and mailings. A good marketing department will spark consumers' interest to the point that they actually go out and buy the darned book. So basically, marketing means doing whatever it takes to get as many books as possible into—and then out of—the stores, and into readers' hands.

Publicity Director: Works with the marketing department to get the word out about new books. Publicists coordinate campaigns that include review submissions, book tours, author events, speaking engagements, online presence, and media interviews. They are generally even more overworked than other people in publishing.

Sales Director: Guides a team of sales representatives in distributing your book to booksellers. Sales reps are the direct liaison to retailers and wholesalers. They are out on the frontlines selling to their accounts, and in most companies their opinions are very influential, because they have their finger on the pulse, or in the pie. They have their finger somewhere.

Art Director: Oversees all art for the publisher, most notably the cover design.

Obviously, this lineup varies greatly from company to company and division to division. For instance, if you're dealing with a tiny publisher there may be only one or two people playing all these roles. At a giant company, there may be twenty or more people in the room. Some may limit attendance to a few key people; others may be more democratic.

THE DRAMA UNFOLDS

There will probably be more than one proposal on the agenda, and poor Barry Samuels will have to sit there pretending to be interested while a young editorial assistant named Rebecca Tweak pitches her first proposal ever—a coffee-table-sized collection of photographs of butter-sculpture busts of American presidents, by the former executive chef of a cruise line. She really believes in this book, and has researched the market and competition titles, but her voice shakes with nerves as she begins her pitch.

"This butter be good," murmurs Mort Meyer, the marketing director, to a cute publicist he's been flirting with all week.

"Fat chance," she giggles. But they both listen politely as Rebecca Tweak completes her pitch.

Strong opinions are expressed in the editorial board meeting, since this is everyone's big chance to weigh in on an important decision—to publish or not to publish. This meeting is one of the arenas in which the publishing house affirms or alters the character of its list, and at times a proposal may lead to a heated discussion of the company's identity and the kind of books it needs to acquire. These discussions influence the decisions made at editorial board; but what many people don't know is that a great proposal (like yours) can influence this ongoing process as well.

After a series of rapid-fire questions from the marketing and publicity directors, along with some grilling about financial projections and reminders of the high cost of publishing photo books from the publisher, Tom Slammit (who had a fight with his wife that morning and is in a cranky mood to begin with), a decision is made to pass on *Churning to Be President: Profiles in Butter*. Rebecca runs from the conference room in tears, as a few less sensitive colleagues whisper jokes about "churning a profit" and her "butter failure."

Next up is another nonfiction proposal, presented by Mimi Bigones, a far more experienced editor, who specializes in self-help titles. *Videology* promotes the idea that—not unlike the concept of astrology—human beings' personalities and preferences are affected by the shows aired on TV at the moment of their birth.

"So," says Bigones, "if you were born during *I Love Lucy*, you might end up spending your life cooking up harebrained schemes and trying to get onstage at the Copacabana; if you were born during *The Sopranos*—well, you get the idea."

Bigones' pitch is brief and perfunctory; when no one in the room responds with enthusiasm she all but admits that she is presenting this book as a favor to the agent, an important player and a lifelong friend, and agrees that it may not be a good fit for the list. She doesn't seem at all ruffled when the book is declined in a matter of minutes. After the meeting ends, she'll immediately place a call to the agent.

"I really went to the wall for *Videology*," Bigones will say, "but we got shot down by Marketing. They just didn't get it. Hey—want to do lunch next Tuesday?"

Now it's Barry Samuels's turn. He clears his throat, adjusts his bifocals, and explains why *When the Sparrow Cries Wolf* is worth publishing. Armed with facts about America's bird-watching-club demographics, he goes to bat for your book. Samuels answers sales director Jane Hankie's questions with a list of retail outlets that cater to bird lovers (provided by the agent, who got it from you), in addition to bookstores specializing in mystery books. He eases the concerns of the marketing and publicity team with an e-mail printout expressing interest from the producer of a national radio show (Ethel Bluestocking makes a point of maintaining contacts in the media), and he seduces the publisher with promises of endorsements from three bestselling authors who love bird watching. Samuels knows this because he is in a bird-watching club with David Sedaris, Joyce Carol Oates, and Toni Morrison.

A heated discussion ensues about your book. Tom, the publisher, still cranky after his difficult morning, isn't sure he wants to take a risk on an unknown author. Marketing director Mort Meyer, an avid mystery reader, longs to beef up this part of the fiction list.

He nudges the sales director, with whom he's had a long, private discussion before the meeting.

"Oh!" Jane says, remembering her cue, "I think this one will fly right off the shelves." Everyone in the room groans, but the mood is lightened.

"I think it's a fresh idea, with a lot of potential. I don't even care about bird watching, but I thought the writing was awesome," says Tina Frisque, one of the publicists. Sometimes they actually do talk about the quality of the writing in these meetings.

"I don't know, I didn't think it was that strong," says Mimi Bigones, who is always competing with Barry Samuels. "It just didn't sing to me. We'd be going head-to-head with some heavy-hitters on the other spring lists. Elmore Leonard has a new one coming out, John Lescroart, Lisa Scottoline . . . and that Agatha Christie anthology . . . ."

"Isn't Agatha Christie dead?" asks Tina Frisque, looking puzzled.

"Yes, honey," replies Leo Palma-Cortes, the art director, "but that doesn't stop Penguin from crankin' out new editions of her books."

"There's no better author than a famous dead one," grumbles Tom Slammit, sending a shudder through Barry Samuels. The publisher seems to be in a bad mood, and one way or another, he has to be on board if Samuels is going to acquire the book.

"You've got a good point—dead authors don't whine!" Veronica Pickle, the publicity director, chuckles.

"I don't know about this," Slammit continues, as he starts checking e-mail on his BlackBerry. "Who the hell cares about bird watching anyway?"

"Sedaris does," Barry Samuels reminds him. "Look at all these." He pulls out a sheaf of papers, printouts of websites for bird watchers. "And Joyce writes a bird-watching blog that gets 2,000 hits a day. You put that together with all of our avid mystery readers, and you've got a sure-fire hit on your hands."

Samuels realizes his reasoning may be a little shaky, but he really wants this one, and he can feel it slipping away, especially when Mimi Bigones raises another concern.

"The title doesn't work for me," she declares. "It's too long. No one will remember it. You need something with more pizzazz."

"What do you mean by 'pizzazz,' Mimi?" Samuels asks, suddenly feeling tired.

"Oh, I don't know. *Maid for Murder* or something."

"How about *Bird on a Wire*?" asks Jane Hankie.

"*Swallow This*?" suggests Leo Palma-Cortes.

The discussion of alternative titles, sales track of similar books, and the merits of the manuscript itself continues for about twenty minutes, until finally Tom Slammit comes around, just enough.

He's still isn't really convinced, but the e-mail he just read from *his* boss contained a mandate from Unimax corporate headquarters to beef up the list by acquiring more titles, and fast. A pretty good writer with an original idea and a completed fiction manuscript could be a valuable commodity, especially since this author isn't in a position to ask for a large advance, even with the legendary Edith Bluestocking representing the property.

"All right, it sounds like some of you really want to do this, but I'm not so sure. If you're going to make me give a hoot about a bunch of bird watchers, I want more sex—and somebody better die right off the bat," Tom Slammit declares.

Barry Samuels sees his chance.

"How about if we ask for a rewrite on the opening chapter, going in the direction Tom is suggesting," he says.

THE PHONE CALL

The meeting is adjourned, and Barry Samuels goes off to deliver the verdict, which isn't really a verdict at all, to Edith Bluestocking. Edith, in turn, calls you.

"Are you okay?" Edith asks. She says this because you started hyperventilating the moment you heard your agent's voice on the phone.

"Sure, I'm fine," you gasp. "What's up?"

"Well," Edith says, "there's good news, but not the news you wanted to hear. Ballpoint is interested, but they want to see a rewrite of the first chapter. They want you to bump up the love interest and have a little more excitement right at the start—preferably in the form of a murder."

You are devastated. You considered your opening chapter to be a masterpiece. Like Mozart, you felt you had everything in its place, just right. However, this is a moment when you need to decide—are you willing to let go of your opinion and submit to the desire of the mysterious, faceless publishing house?

Of course you are. You are a rookie author and you want to get published.

"Actually," says Edith Bluestocking, "if Barry Samuels goes for the rewrite you'll be in excellent hands. He's a very good editor, and your book will be the better for it. And Leo Palma-Cortes is the best art director in the business. It's bound to look gorgeous, too."

You thank Edith and say your goodbyes. Then you make a pot of coffee, turn on your computer, and try to think of someone to kill, preferably in the middle of having hot sex, in the first chapter.

BOTTOM LINE

Whether or not a manuscript gets accepted can depend on the trends in the marketplace, corporate directives (at a big publisher), the publisher's mission, goals, and financial considerations, your agent's connections, and other factors beyond your control. Your job: be a pro and do the best job you can on the part of the process that's within your control. Then say a prayer to the gods of Talent, Luck, and Timing, and hope for the best.

CHAPTER SEVEN

YOU AND YOUR EDITOR

Here's help for the lucky author whose book has been acquired by a publisher and some tips for negotiating the author-editor relationship. Be prepared to change your title and let go of those preconceived notions about your cover.

There's been a rumor going around for a while now that the venerable old publishing model of an acquiring editor actually editing your book has gone the way of the typewriter and the record player. As with all rumors, there is some element of truth to this, but from what we've experienced there are still a lot of editors out there who are willing to roll up their sleeves, sharpen their pencils, and get to work on your manuscript.

ALL MANUSCRIPTS NEED EDITING

Although it's true that many agents have taken on more of an editorial role in order to present proposals and manuscripts that are as salable as possible, this has more to do with the fact that so many people want to be published.

Tough Love from the Author Enablers

Just because you have a great computer and the most up-to-date word processing software and templates, there's no substitute for good writing, rewriting, and editing. Remember— Shakespeare wrote with a pen and Homer was blind. ‹ ‹‹

Aspiring writers have access to computers and word processing programs that make it physically easier to produce a decent-looking manuscript, so there's more competition in sheer quantity than ever before. A good editor (and most of them, let's face it, wouldn't have jobs if they weren't pretty good) *will* edit your book. There may be moments when this won't be a lot of fun, because you thought (once again) that you were done. But it is your editor's job to look at the big picture—the work as a whole, consistency of voice, the narrative arc (that the story flows and makes sense), that it is structured properly, that it isn't overwritten or missing crucial components, and that it is a fresh, original work. And it is the editor's job (along with the managing editor) to comb through the book, line by line, helping you shape your writing into the masterpiece we all know it was meant to be.

But editors do a lot more than edit. For one thing, sometimes they take you to lunch, often at very nice restaurants. You'll be too worried about the possibility of spilling something or getting spinach stuck in your teeth to actually *enjoy* the lunch, but this is something editors are good at, so try to have some fun.

Just as important, at most publishing companies it is the editors who acquire the books. Most of them don't have the authority to make an offer without jumping through some company/corporate hoops, but these are the people who are actually charged with finding and buying intellectual property on behalf of the publisher, taking on a kind of parental role over your manuscript. Since you've probably spent years writing your book and undoubtedly think of it as your baby, this can take some getting used to. Once a publisher acquires your book, it really isn't all yours anymore. As in any co-parenting arrangement, the two of you may not always agree on the judgment calls. Choose your battles carefully, and be willing to compromise. Understanding the process from the editor's point of view can help make this a smooth and positive relationship, and—in some cases—even an enduring friendship.

Editors are inundated with submissions, and every editor comes into work each day to find a new stack of manuscripts and proposals. They are all looking out for books in their area of interest or expertise, and they are trying to avoid books that are too similar to something else the house has recently bought or published, as well as books by fanatics, lunatics, and terrible writers. Above all, they are looking for books that they think they can sell to their colleagues in-house, who will then sell to the sales reps, who will then sell to the retailers, who will sell your book to readers.

A MADE-UP TRUE-LIFE ACCOUNT OF THE EDITORIAL PROCESS

Editor Laura is staring at a pile of manuscripts on her desk. Loretta, Laura's underpaid assistant, has made some notes on each manuscript, but Laura knows enough not to entirely trust her assistant's views, as Loretta is more focused on checking her Facebook page and managing her boyfriend's alternative polka band than on her work. Still, Loretta is cheerful, shows up on time, and somehow manages to live on a pathetically small salary, so Laura feels she can't really complain.

Laura flips through the stack and something about Tony's novel catches her eye. "Vampire dogs," she thinks. "No one's done that before."

Laura starts reading Tony's book that night and really enjoys it. She plans on reading more the next day, forgetting that she has back-to-back meetings to discuss books she's already working on. Other burning issues arise, and before she knows it weeks pass and Tony's manuscript still sits, neglected but not forgotten.

Eventually Tony's agent calls Laura to talk about the latest movies, catch up on some publishing gossip, compliment Laura for doing a great job on another client's book, and, by the way, see how it's going with Tony's submission. Laura, looking at the unfinished manuscript on her shelf, is evasive. But that night she takes the manuscript home and finishes reading it. There are a couple of weaknesses—nothing that can't be fixed—and she wants to make an offer. Meanwhile Tony, feeling like a loser because no one has bought his book yet, fills out an application to work as a character actor at Disneyland. He's thinking he'd make a good Goofy.

The next day, Laura starts laying the groundwork for Tony's book. Keep in mind that buying a book is a serious gamble for the publisher, who will be committing money, staff time, and reputation to a book that may sell only a small number of copies. A consensus that Tony's book is worthy must be reached within the company before an offer can be made, and a lot of water-cooler politicking can occur. Laura starts by talking the novel up to some key people, and also asks a few colleagues to read an excerpt from one of the stronger chapters.

Some days go by, and now there is a small chorus of voices agreeing that this book may have potential. The editorial director—AKA Laura's boss—backs the book, and so does the publisher. Laura has been given the thumbs-up to make an offer—nothing extravagant, but a real commitment.

Tony gets the call from his agent and gets out of bed for the first time in days. However, a deal has not been struck—in fact, it will probably take weeks of back-and-forth between Laura (and her bosses) and Tony's agent before they strike a deal. When Tony gets the word that the terms of the sale are basically finalized, he goes to Disneyland to celebrate. While the contract is being drawn up, introductions are made. Tony talks to Laura and perhaps a few other members of the publishing team. He is ecstatic. He loves them all.

HURRY UP AND WAIT

What Tony doesn't realize is that it may be two years before he is a published author. Laura has plenty of other books to work on and more projects to acquire. She also has to work with the marketing and publicity teams on books that have been recently published or are coming out in the next season, and she has to maintain her relationships with the agents, authors, and other publishing pros that are the lifeblood of her work—this is why she's so good at taking people to lunch. Plus, she has a life. Sometimes.

When Laura does get around to editing Tony's book, she suggests some serious structural changes. She thinks it should begin with a scene that now appears in the middle of the book. She doesn't like Tony's humorous sidebars, something he worked really hard on but that she considers inappropriate in a vampire dog novel. She thinks the scenes with the primary female human character are weak and two-dimensional and need beefing up. But the really upsetting news for Tony is that Laura wants to change the title. Her suggestion—*Barking for Blood*—horrifies Tony, who calls his agent to complain. The agent, accustomed to upset authors, calms Tony down by agreeing with a lot of what he says. Actually, she thinks that his original title, *Canine Revenge,* didn't work; but she doesn't think *Barking for Blood* works either. She thinks it should be *Old Fangful.*

Over the next year, Laura and Tony go through several drafts together. By the time they are done it is practically another book. The funny thing is, Tony begins to see that their work is improving his writing. He's even come around about the new title, *Count Barkula.* But when Laura says she is happy with the latest version Tony is surprised and concerned. What about the typos? Laura calms him down by explaining that the book is now going to the managing editorial department for copyediting and design.

Several months later Tony receives a printed copy of his manuscript littered with tiny red marks. Copyeditors are grammar fanatics, happiest when they find errors that need correcting—and they *always* find errors. They actually *like* finding errors. That's why they have the job.

Tony has to be in New York for a family visit, so he makes an appointment to stop in at the publisher's office and meet Laura in person for the first time.

Facing the large Midtown building that houses his publisher's offices, Tony has to stop for a minute to catch his breath. He can hardly believe this is happening! He walks through security and wills himself to remember every moment of the elevator ride up to the fifteenth-floor editorial offices; the smooth, carpeted ride; the genteel bell announcing the elevator's arrival on his floor; the polka-dot blouse on the young receptionist who asks him to take a seat. He looks around and sees posters advertising books he's read and enlarged photographs of some of his favorite authors. He feels his life changing as he sits there, and vows to write about this moment in his next novel.

Laura appears, and Tony is momentarily startled—he had always pictured her as a tall brunette with glasses, and instead he sees a petite blonde. It will take him a few more meetings to remember what Laura really looks like when he talks to her on the phone.

After a quick tour of the office, Laura offers Tony a couple of hot-off-the-presses hardcovers to read on the plane, and he's thrilled to accept. She then calls a few colleagues, and they gather in Laura's office before going to lunch.

THE TRANSITION FROM EDITORIAL TO MARKETING AND PUBLICITY

The purpose of the lunch is to get acquainted in person, of course, but it is also something we like to call the "hand-off lunch," in which Tony is introduced to the people who will guide him through the next stage of the publishing process. He doesn't realize it yet, but his direct communication with Laura will lessen as his book gets closer to publication. She'll move on to other books, and he'll work more closely with the publicity and marketing people. This can be a difficult transition, kind of like a parent handing a toddler over to the babysitter and trying to leave the house as the child clings to his mother's neck. When done skillfully, though, the hand-off is a seamless, positive experience. (Of course, it doesn't have to be lunch. It can be, and often is, a phone-and-e-mail hand-off. But we like lunch.)

Laura is a pro, and Tony is impressed with Veronica and Ben, the publicity and marketing team assigned to his title. They've come well-prepared with a creative plan for getting the word out about Tony's book, and invite him to contribute ideas. They also ask him to fill out something called an author questionnaire.

The questionnaire is an extensive document that asks about the author's background, affiliations, and experience. It's not a whole lot of fun to fill out, but it's important, as it gives the publicity team crucial information about the author's contacts and platform, where he comes from, and who his people are. Tony is also asked to write a ten-question "dream interview": the ten questions he would most like to be asked about his book, followed by the answers. You will have already done this, because you read our book. This may be used in his press kit, and might even appear published in a secondary-market publication as an interview. It helps the publicist refine the pitch and figure out how to approach the media, and clarifies what questions an author is most comfortable answering.

For the next few months Tony is working with Veronica, Ben, and some of the others in the publicity department. A publicist gets in touch about his personal travel plans; there's no budget for a tour, but the organizer of a vampire film festival and dog show in Austin is wondering about an author appearance. The marketing team wants some information. At the same time the copyeditor is being a pest with all kinds of niggling detail questions.

Tough Love from the Author Enablers

So you think you have quite a sense of design and you've always pictured the cover of your vampire dog book as all black. What could be more dramatic? Take our word for it—you should let your publisher design your cover. We can't guarantee that they'll get it perfect, but they are the pros and they have both the experience and the objectivity that you lack. We can often tell at a glance when a book has been self-published, because the cover never quite has that professionally designed look. ‹ ‹‹

Laura is still on the job, checking on everything and approving every stage of the book's progress. She writes his cover copy, fights for a better marketing plan, and argues with everyone about the cover images. She is talking the book up in-house and to colleagues in the business.

PUB DATE: AT LAST, IT'S A REAL BOOK

Finally Tony's publication date is approaching. The reviews in the trade publications (such as *Publisher's Weekly*) are positive. The publicist tells him there's "a nice buzz starting" with independent booksellers. Tony imagines little bees buzzing around his neighborhood bookstore, and wonders if his next book should be about vampire bees.

The pub date finally arrives! (Pub date, you no doubt gathered, is short for the publication date. See our handy glossary for more on this and other publishing lingo.) Tony comes home from work and throws his Goofy head down on the floor, almost hitting the lovely fruit basket sent by his publisher to mark the day. He checks his messages and carefully goes over the itinerary sent by his publicity team—some readings in local bookstores over the next few weeks, several phoned-in radio interviews, and one trip out of town. Thanks to Laura's efforts, the publisher found money in the budget to send him to that vampire/dog show event in Austin after all.

Tony takes a drive down to his local bookstore, and there it is, right on the New Fiction table, five copies of his first published book . . . next to a huge stack of John Grisham novels.

No, the world doesn't stop for Tony's publication date. But he's now a legitimate published author with a new book that has "buzz"—and he has Laura to thank, in large part, for that. He has yet to experience his first fan letter, or the first time he sees a stranger reading his book on an airplane. Those will be wonderful moments, but none is quite as lovely as seeing his book on the New Fiction table for the very first time.

IF THINGS DON'T TURN OUT TO BE PERFECT (AND WHEN HAVE THEY EVER?)

In a less-perfect scenario, Tony's editor might not be as competent or attentive . . . or might leave the company altogether in the middle of Tony's book's publication process. When an editor leaves mid-book (to keep the parental metaphor going) the book and author are described as "orphaned" and it's not a good thing. The new editor won't have the same level of interest in a project she did not acquire, and may even see some value in its failure. If an editor is inattentive or simply incompetent (or clearly too busy with that John Grisham title to care much about yours), you won't be as lucky as Tony.

There are some things you can do to remedy these situations, and they have to do with—go figure—graciousness, charm, and walking the line between being a good communicator and a pest.

In a best-case scenario, your original editor would let her authors know that she is leaving and put you in touch with her replacement. When you are introduced to your new editor (either in person or by phone or e-mail), propose an in-person meeting if that's possible. Do what you can to develop a good relationship; then get out of the way. If you feel like your concerns are not being addressed, or worse, this would be a good time to ask your agent to act as your advocate and get you a little more attention from the editorial department. Most of all, trust the process and don't take your frustrations out on your new editor just because your old editor decided to move, or go to graduate school, or run for president, or something.

With an editor who simply isn't good at his job, if you can afford the extra expense you might want to enlist the aid of a professional book doctor or freelance editor, just to make sure your book is the best it can be. However, it's worth noting that the in-house editor has the final say on edits, and the publisher could end up rejecting a freelance editor's changes. But please don't assume that these unhappy scenarios will be the case.

BOTTOM LINE

Most editors are true professionals who really care, who will do the very best they can to help your book succeed, and who will still be working at the same house when you are shopping your second manuscript. And we firmly believe there's no book in the world that doesn't benefit from the intelligent and judicious attention of a skilled, experienced editor.

CHAPTER EIGHT

MARKETING AND PUBLICITY: GETTING THE WORD OUT

Large publishing companies have in-house publicity departments, and the time will come when you'll be weaned from the editorial team and handed over to marketing and publicity. There are many ways you can help your publicist do the best possible job, and a lot you can do on your own, too.

What the heck *is* marketing, and how do you do it for your own book? We'll try to provide a simple overview to this complicated question.

But before we discuss marketing and publicity, we want to make it clear that the most important thing you can ever do for your book is write a great manuscript. A wonderful book makes everyone's job easier. The sales people want to sell it, media producers want to book the author, and booksellers are enthusiastic. But what is a great manuscript? Now, for another twist: instead of thinking only about how beautiful or revolutionary or clever your writing is or how intensive or groundbreaking your research is or the reasons why your book is destined to become a classic, think instead about who your audience is, why anyone should pick up your book (or click on it online) and buy it. Why would a bookseller steer someone to your book? Why would a producer be interested in you? It is this combination—a timely manuscript on a subject of interest by a qualified, talented, disciplined author— that makes for a terrific, successful manuscript. Write a good book, because a great marketing plan will not always overcome mediocrity.

MARKETING

The goal of marketing is to ignite a word-of-mouth campaign so that your book will begin to take on a life of its own. Without this, interest in the book will die out and the publisher will, logically, move on to the next project. The hard truth is that most books don't make enough money to warrant the publisher keeping the title in print and many don't reach the point where the publisher starts paying the author royalties, which can only happen if the book has "earned out" (more about this later—also, see the glossary). Publishers make their money on the minority of books that succeed.

We're not trying to discourage you. In fact, we are trying to encourage you to take your writing and your role as author seriously enough that you challenge your own preconceptions about this process. What kind of book are you best suited to write? If you want your book to lead the pack, you must write in a genre and deliver a manuscript that suits you as an author, in terms of both your talent and skills and your background and education (formal and informal—for some books, for instance, time spent in prison can come in handy), and write on a subject for which there is an audience, in a manner that communicates your story and message. All this is to give yourself the best possible shot at finding the readers who will buy your book.

In a trade publishing house—one that publishes for the general consumer market—the marketing department develops materials designed to help the sales force get orders from retailers. These materials include catalogue copy, cover design, in-store displays, advertising, online presence, giveaways and promotions, outreach to organizations and mailings, and anything else they can come up with to get attention in a crowded market.

HOW MARKETING WORKS

Here's how it usually works: after a book is acquired by a publisher, a publicity and marketing plan and budget are put together before the manuscript is completed. Plans can change, but the initial budget is based on such factors as sales projections and early media interest. Your company-assigned publicist will start sending out copies of your book to reviewers several months before your publication date. These can be in the form of a simply bound manuscript, galleys or advance readers copies (ARCs), or finished books. Once the book is in stores you'll have about six more weeks of her attention before she has to move on to other projects. Keep in mind that this publicist is working on several other books at the same time, has to go to way too many meetings, and in the case of first-time authors is working with a very small budget.

There are ways to supplement your publisher's efforts. Several months before publication, ransack your address book and provide names and addresses of your personal media contacts and any authors or prominent people you know who might give you endorsements; set up some book-signing events in areas where you know a lot of people who are likely to show up; and let your publicist know when and where you plan to be traveling on your own, in case there's media or bookstore interest in other cities.

Tough Love from the Author Enablers

Don't bug or harass or whine at your publicist to the point where she has to spend so much time talking to you that she doesn't have time to publicize your book, and might even grow to dislike you. Be polite, friendly, and informative, but don't use her as a punching bag or therapist. The more time she has to spend talking you down, the less time she'll have to work on your book. ‹ ‹‹

We can't overemphasize how important it is to determine the demographics of the audience for your book (twelve- to fourteen-year-old girls and their moms, middle-aged football fans, armchair archeologists, etc.). A clear sense of the audience will help your marketing and publicity team as they develop the appropriate materials.

MORE WAYS YOU CAN HELP MARKET YOURSELF

Maintaining your web presence is a low-cost and effective means for getting the word out about your book, upcoming appearances, reviews, and so on, so make sure you have an appealing book-related website, whether or not you, your publisher, or both of you are handling updates and maintenance.

Watch the news for opportunities to present yourself as an expert to local and national media outlets. Remind your publicist that you can be called upon to comment on breaking stories. Always make sure you have a copy of your book on hand, even when you travel. Keep networking, and look for opportunities to participate in group readings with other authors—which is, by the way, one of many good reasons to be nice to and maintain contact with your colleagues.

PUBLICITY

As you come close to your publication date, the publicity element of your book's campaign kicks in. There is no sharp line between marketing and publicity; the two are different approaches to the same goal: getting attention for your book so it will sell.

THE PROS AND CONS (AND TIMING) OF HIRING YOUR OWN PUBLICIST

Many authors consider hiring an independent publicist to supplement the efforts of the in-house publicity team. Knowing that most in-house publicists are working on several projects at a time and have a limited window in which to concentrate on any title, this can be a great idea—but there are several factors to consider before making this commitment, which can be an expensive proposition since it will most likely mean shelling out money from your own pocket.

It doesn't make a lot of sense to hire a publicist once your book is released, and many of the best independent publicists will not consider signing on to a project unless they have the opportunity to do so well in advance of the pub date. For example, long-lead magazines choose their content at least four months in advance, and you want to coordinate the coverage of your book to fall into the crucial window between the time your book goes on sale and two months later, when the publisher and the world begin to move on. This time frame varies with different types of books, but in general those first two months are when a lot of things are going to happen—in other words, it's show time.

Then there's this simple fact of (human) nature: if your assigned in-house publicist knows that you've hired someone else to do the heavy lifting, he may be tempted to concentrate on other projects with the limited time available.

Still, the right publicist, hired well in advance of the pub date, can do wonders for a book. It depends on you, the subject matter of your book, your comfort level with the in-house marketing plan, and your budget. We don't recommend taking out a second mortgage to finance your publicity campaign, but if you have the extra bucks handy then the investment might make sense. For instance, let's say you are an aspiring children's book author who has written the *Boopsie and Wigglebottom* adventure series, and you also just met a publicist who is a genius at publicizing children's books. In this situation, by all means, hire the publicist.

In the best of all scenarios, the freelance publicist will work well with your in-house team, everyone will supplement and enhance each others' efforts, and you, Boopsie, and Wigglebottom will hit one out of the park.

PLAN AHEAD

Whether you're thinking about publicity or any other aspect of your publishing journey, it's crucial to remember that by the time a book is published it is too late to make suggestions or complain or decide to hire a publicist or, really, take any action at all that will affect the publicity campaign at or close to the on-sale date. (The on-sale date is the term used in publishing for, duh, the date the book officially goes on sale. Sometimes retailers ignore this date and sell early, but they're not supposed to.) Decisions are made and budgets are set long before this time comes, and that's why it's important to meet your deadlines and communicate with your publisher every step of the way.

Nine Tips for Helping Your Publicist Do a Great Job

Your book, *Light Bulb: Twenty-Seven Steps to Business Brilliance*, is about to be published by Cranky Pants Press, and you couldn't be happier. You've been assigned a publicist who is bright and pleasant, even if she appears to be just out of junior high. Here's what you can do to help her do a great job for you and your book:

1. Provide an author photo, one-page bio, and a Q&A (a list of the ten questions you'd most like to be asked, along with the answers).

2. Provide copies of any press you've received in advance of the book's release. A profile in the local paper or online, video of a cable TV interview, that time you were on morning radio—this could all be useful in pitching bigger and better interviews.

3. Provide a list of your personal media and bookseller connections and any appropriate mailing lists. If the president of the NBC affiliate in your town happens to be your wife's second cousin, now is the time to call in a favor. Friends will enjoy knowing where and when you'll be appearing.

4. Provide a "big mouth" list of influential people in your field. Your editor will want to ask them for endorsements. Your publicist may want to use these endorsements in your book's press materials. Endorsements from others in your field help the publisher "position" the book in the marketplace. The idea is to find the appropriate audience, readers who are predisposed to like you. Endorsements carry a lot more weight with publishers and booksellers than you'd think—probably a lot more than they should.

5. Let your publicist know if you set up your own interviews. This is important for two reasons: you'll avoid double-booking, and she will be able to add your appearances to her marketing notes—the bump in sales after your literary lunch appearance in Dallas will make sense. If the sales dip instead of bump, then you should stop doing literary lunches, right?

6. Communicate with your publicist, share ideas and contacts, but don't drive her crazy. Give her time to get her work done. Call once in a while just to say hi and check in.

7. Don't forget to say thank you. A little kindness and appreciation go a long way.

8. Trust the process. Things won't happen as quickly as you would like. But you know what? Your publicist probably didn't forget to send your book to *Oprah*, *Fresh Air*, or the *New York Times*, if it was appropriate to do so. Really.

9. Understand that at some point, your publicist will have to move on to the next project. There are many ways you can keep momentum going on your own, and if you have a great relationship with your publicist, you can get lots of help during this transition.

Finally, remember the Author Enablers' top secret trick for getting the most out of your publicist: send an occasional box of chocolates. Remember, publicists are pros—some more experienced and dedicated than others—but it's their job, and they're doing their best. Let's hope this is the first of many books you'll be writing; if that plan works out (or even if it doesn't) it makes sense to build good relationships with the publishing professionals you meet along the way. Not every book is a hit, but there is such a thing as a career built on modest successes. Hang in there.

THE BOOK TOUR

Every author dreams of going on a book tour—until it actually happens. Book tours do look like fun: free travel to exciting cities; great hotel rooms, expenses paid; appearances on radio and television; reading from your work to standing-room-only crowds in beautiful bookstores; and the attentive care of professional media escorts, assigned to handle the logistics of your day.

If you've been to an event featuring a very popular author you've probably noticed the large audiences and the solicitous attention

MARKETING AND PUBLICITY: GETTING THE WORD OUT   113

lavished on the guest of honor, who is whisked away at the first sign of fatigue. For you, the first-time author on your first book tour, reality might be a little different.

First of all, we should emphasize that book tours aren't as popular as they used to be. There are several reasons for this. Media deregulation and other economic factors have changed the landscape for everyone. There used to be a lot more local media around—and therefore more need for and interest in touring authors—than there is now. A typical book-tour day might begin with a local morning TV show such as *People Are Talking*, then an hour on a call-in radio show, followed by lunch with a journalist. The afternoon might consist of another appearance on local TV—a brief segment either at the end of the news or on one of the weekly magazine-format interview shows—and end with an evening reading and signing in a bookstore. But the media bookings would be the anchor of the tour, the reason an author was sent to one city rather than another.

As media moved toward syndication, the *Good Morning America* type shows came to dominate, while locally produced shows declined. At the same time newspapers also decreased in number and viability (especially around the book-review section). As a result, book tours have become more focused on bookstores and less on media. This would have been okay if independent bookstores were thriving as community cultural centers, because the need for authors could replace the dwindling supply of local media when it came time for the publishers to decide where to send an author. But the number of independent bookstores is currently in decline, and without the heavy-duty all-day event promotion offered by multiple media appearances, it's harder to get bodies into the stores to hear an author read. There are still a number of great independent bookstores and these have devised their own marketing methods for drawing crowds, some very successful, but weighed against rising travel costs and shrinking budgets, publishers have moved away from touring for many of their authors.

The growing importance of online media also has a lot to do with the waning book tour. Authors can easily contribute articles, participate in interviews and blogs, and even meet their fans without ever leaving home.

Book tours still exist, but they can no longer be expected—especially for first-time authors. And you shouldn't necessarily be disappointed. Remember, the point of book tours was never for authors to enjoy airport cuisine and adventures in Cleveland; it was to sell books and get the author's name out there. If there are better strategies for accomplishing these goals, wouldn't you rather these be employed? Also, book tours aren't necessarily that much fun. They can be lonely, frustrating, and difficult, especially for authors who aren't well-known enough (yet) to guarantee that they'll draw a crowd.

BE PREPARED

If you are sent on a book tour, be prepared for a wide variety of experiences, some of which are bound to be disappointing. You'll find yourself at loose ends in a city where you know no one, or booked solid in the place where you have a close friend with no time to visit. You might find bookstores where everything was done right—an article in the paper, a great display, a flattering newsletter listing—and still no one shows up to hear you read. (This can even happen to famous authors.) On the other hand, you'll also find delightful surprises where one might expect disaster. A double-booking ("Yikes! Two authors with the word 'shoes' in the titles of their new novels were accidentally scheduled to read on the same night. Oops!") might, if handled with humor and imagination, lead to a terrific twofer event, and a new fellow-author friend made later over dinner. The dream of luxury travel and hotels will play out in long security lines and missed connections. We've heard a story of one author who, after long delays, checked into her hotel room late at night with only a few hours to sleep until her early morning wake-up call. She got into her nightie, brushed her teeth, and only then discovered that she'd been booked into a room that didn't have a bed! In other words, it will be exactly as much fun as any other kind of travel, minus your loved ones.

The marketing and publicity team are the ones who arrange author tours. Generally the budget is small, and as a first-time author you may find yourself staying in relatives' guest rooms, speaking in near-empty bookstores, and pondering the point of it all.

DIFFERENT TYPES OF BOOK TOURS—INCLUDING CREATING YOUR OWN

The tour may take any number of forms. A traditional tour might be two weeks of travel, flights from city to city, author appearances once, twice, or more a day. You may do a phone-in radio show in the morning and another that afternoon, and stop at one store to sign a pile of books while on your way to another bookstore to speak that evening. Two weeks of this can be exhausting and costs the publisher a lot of money. Another type of tour may be down-and-dirty, consisting of the city where you live and one other you can get to cheaply and easily.

Often there is no tour, and many ambitious authors overcome the limitations of their publishers' budgets by using their own speaking engagements as book promotion opportunities. If you're going to travel anyway, contact your publisher well in advance to see if a book event might be scheduled around your trip. You tell your publicist that you are going to Poughkeepsie for a work conference. You or your employer are paying for the travel, room, and board. Taking advantage of this situation, the publicist arranges for a media event or bookstore appearance, or both. Publicists call this a "tie-in" tour, meaning events are scheduled to tie in to travel that is already planned and paid for, but not by the publisher.

Another way to work the book-tour system is to find a group or organization other than your publisher, your employer, or yourself to pay your way. We happen to know about Jewish book festivals from personal experience, as Kathi's publisher used Jewish book festival bookings to supplement a tour for her first novel.

Here's how those festivals work. During the fall pre-holiday season, synagogues and Jewish community centers (JCCs) in many cities sponsor their own book festivals, to which they invite Jewish authors and/or authors of books that are of Jewish interest. The lovely thing about these events is that the organizers have figured out ways to cover travel expenses, so, with enough advance planning, a clever publisher can piggyback additional stops onto a JCC tour. The festivals themselves are well-supported and well-attended, the authors are treated like celebrities, and the seasonal timing guarantees that book sales will be strong. We've heard of other, similar opportunities in niche circuits: culinary schools for cookbook authors, corporate conferences and retreats, academic and clergy conferences, clown academies, and the like. Keep your eyes peeled for groups that might be a good fit for your book, and watch out for those funny little cars.

Although it's unlikely that you'll get your expenses paid by the organizers, it's worth pursuing bookings at established book festivals of any kind. Even if you're not the big draw, even if—weekend after weekend—you find yourself sitting at a book-signing table *next to* the guy with the 200-person line, after you've autographed five books as slowly and carefully as possible, even if you're placed on a panel that makes no sense in terms of the theme of your book, these events are worth it for the sheer number of people who attend and the inter-author networking opportunities. Most book festivals give preference to authors with recently published books, some (especially if you happen to be just the thing they're looking for to round out a panel) will come up with a room for a night or two if you can get yourself to town, and many festivals have volunteers available to drive authors to and from events. There's always a green room where snacks are provided, other authors are milling around, and everyone is wearing a name tag. Think about it: would you rather be sitting alone in a bookstore waiting for someone to walk in and ask for a signed book, or sitting next to a bestselling author whose fans are entertaining to watch, even if they're not there for you? Maybe next year, next book, they *will* be there for you. In the meantime, you can watch every move Mr. Bestseller Guy makes and pick up a few tips.

Some Tips for Surviving Your Book Tour
Travel:

- Amy Tan says, "Bring your dog (under eleven pounds) and you'll never be lonely."
- Rita Mae Brown says, "Send a Fed-Ex package home every couple of days, with the stuff you don't need anymore."
- Barbara Kingsolver says, "Always find something to do or see that is unique to the area, even if you only have five extra minutes, so you'll remember where you've been."
- Robert Fulghum says, "If you want to be left alone on an airplane, tell your seatmate that you're an accountant for a dog food company." ("Amway distributor" works, too.)
- Try to use carry-on, rather than checked, luggage.
- If you have to check luggage, keep essentials (medicine, your dogs, and—most important—a copy of your book, etc.) with you at all times.
- If you're arriving early in the day, call the hotel and try to arrange an early check-in.
- Keep a complete itinerary with you at all times and let people know if you miss a connection, or if there's some other problem that's going to make you late for an interview.

Wardrobe, etc.:

- Remember—on TV they never shoot below the waist (because that would be unsportsmanlike), and at readings you're usually behind a podium. Leave your fancy shoes home; wear something comfortable. Use your precious suitcase space for tops and accessories.
- If you care about makeup on TV, find out ahead of time if they'll do your makeup at the studio. If they don't (and many don't), run into a department store, buy a lipstick and let the

saleswoman give you a makeover. Your makeup will be perfect for television. (This tip from Dave Barry.)

- Bring spray freshener for your clothes. You might not have time to get them cleaned. One old trick: you can "iron" things by hanging them in the steamy bathroom created by a hot shower.

Health and Fitness

- Tell your publisher that you have low blood sugar and will faint if you don't get to eat lunch. Get a doctor to write you a note if necessary.
- Take vitamins, especially if you are the author of a health and nutrition guide.
- Drink LOTS of water.
- Book tours are no time for concentrated health regimens like diets or quitting smoking. Do that stuff before you leave, and allow yourself some treats. Touring is stressful and hard, and comfort food helps. Ask your grandma if you don't believe us. If your grandma is on book tour, she'd love to hear from you.
- If you have a choice, and appearances are close to each other, walk, don't drive. Fresh air and a little exercise will keep your energy up. Ask your gym teacher.
- Don't expect to get much sleep.

Getting Along with Your Publisher:

- If you meet your company's sales reps, follow up with a nice note thanking them for working so hard to sell your book, and an autographed copy. These folks, along with the booksellers, are the ones who can make your book a success. Don't whine in their presence—save that for therapy, or the dog-food company accountant sitting next to you on the plane.

- Especially if you are a first-time author, try not to have unrealistic expectations. Everyone at your publishing company is overworked, underpaid, and stressed out. Most love books and are doing the best they can to promote yours. Even if that's not the case, it doesn't help to be a jerk. This book may be the most important thing to YOU, but don't lose perspective—focus on ways you can help the cause.
- Try to get your schedule in advance, but don't be surprised if things change at the last minute. (Note—this will ALWAYS happen in the one city where you've arranged to meet an old friend for dinner. It will never happen in the cities where you're lonely and don't know anyone.)
- You don't have to do anything unreasonable or stupid, but if your publisher asks for something, try to accommodate any request quickly and graciously.

The Bookstore:
- If a lot of people show up, be gracious and make eye contact with everyone in line, but help the staff keep things moving. It's bad form to complain about too many people—most authors would love to have your problem!
- If no one, or very few people show up, try to look like you're having fun anyway. Sign stock, look busy, chat with the store employees. If you sit there looking depressed and miserable, no one will want to talk to you.
- Remember that you have a lifelong relationship with books, writing, and bookstores. Don't focus on how many books you sell on a given night. Booksellers are on the front lines of the industry, and they should be a priority for you. Your presence contributes to a valuable community resource, and, if the booksellers like you, they will sell your books for years and years to come.

- When reading, pick a passage that's short and entertaining. It doesn't have to be your best writing—choose something that reads well out loud. Reading is a performance. Practice in front of your friends, read out loud to yourself. If you have to, get "intensive karaoke bar training" to overcome stage fright and learn how to use a microphone and perform in front of people.
- If a really small group shows up, make the event informal— sit in a circle and talk. Half the people there will be aspiring writers—ask them about their work.
- If you are nervous, be honest and funny about it.
- Don't drink alcohol till after the reading. If you never drink, don't drink then, either.
- If the sales reps show up, and you have time, invite them out for a drink or a snack after the reading.
- If the bookseller offers you a book to take home, don't pick the most expensive one in the store.
- When you get home, send thank-you notes to the booksellers.

VIRTUAL TOURS

Another very cost-effective, if lonelier, method of touring is the satellite tour, or phone-in tour. These are set up by pros who specialize in booking authors on morning-drive radio shows and TV programs on network-affiliated stations. For TV, the author goes to one studio, sits in front of a seamless backdrop, and gets beamed in to one TV station after another to do brief interviews with local hosts and news anchors. The tricky part is remembering each interviewer's name, and whether or not you already said that funny thing about the kazoo, the rubber chicken, and the whipped cream to this guy or the last one.

Radio tours are a little more casual for the obvious reason that no one can see you. You can do radio tours in your pajamas, in the bathtub, or in bed. But we recommend getting dressed and sitting up straight like the competent professional you are, because if you're lying down you'll sound less perky. And radio loves perky.

You also might want to have someone with you to help, as the timing on these interviews can be tight. If booked solid, they start at around 7:00 A.M. Eastern time, and end mid-morning West Coast time, with a different call every five or ten minutes, moving geographically from east to west. Radio tours work best if you have two phone lines going, and someone (often the publicist will arrange for an experienced someone) making the next call as you're winding up the last one. The helper can also cue you when time is running out. Radio and satellite tours can give an author national exposure in a few hours, and are a viable alternative for some books and authors.

There are also blog tours, which (obviously) involve sitting in front of your computer typing. These can be arranged through online marketing services for a fee.

MEDIA ESCORTS

One more thing: if you do go on a tour and your publisher offers you the services of a media escort, say yes. Media escorting is a profession known only by publishers and authors who've been on book tours—and the people who do it are a special breed. A good escort will not only drive you to all your interviews and appearances without getting lost, but will brief you on the way:

"The host of the morning show plays poker on Tuesday night; since today is Wednesday, watch out. We'll be able to see in a second if he's won or lost, and how much he drank." "This guy is a thoughtful interviewer but a little dry." "Expect a lot of interruptions for commercial breaks."

You get the idea. The best escorts are charming, engaging, intelligent, well-read people who are resourceful enough to troubleshoot any problem that comes up. They also know all the secret routes and places to park.

If you have family in town, by all means invite them to your book signing and plan to get together for dinner, but let the media escort pick you up at the airport and drive you around. We promise you won't be sorry.

BOTTOM LINE

All of this marketing and publicity stuff may seem a far cry from the pure act of writing that led you here in the first place. But if you want to be an author you have to play your part in the machinery of selling the books. So brush your teeth, smile, be a nice person, show up on time, and do the best job you can.

CHAPTER NINE

THE PROS AND CONS OF SELF-PUBLISHING

Print-on-demand technology is changing the publishing landscape, and no one is sure where it's all going. For the right author, self-publishing can be a viable option, but unless a lot of other things are in place, you'll end up with a pile of books in your garage.

In the beginning there was nothing BUT self-publishing. A writer was a printer was a publisher. But as the universe cooled, these roles gradually separated. In time, authors were seen as effete intellectual snobs who stayed in their rooms churning out genius prose before dying young of consumption, or old of bitterness. The publishers were the rich people in tweed jackets in large urban centers who drank and smoked a lot, and printers were gruff but intelligent ink-spattered sorts.

I DID IT MY WAY: NONTRADITIONAL PUBLISHING

These days the line between author and publisher is blurring once again, as in biblical times. Some authors choose to go the self-publishing route: paying for and handling all aspects of publishing themselves, including marketing, publicity, sales, distribution, and storage. Although self-publishing—that is, the publishing of books by the authors of those works, rather than by established publishers—has been present in one form or another since the beginning of publishing, there has been a marked increase in authors choosing this route. Some of this change is driven by new technologies. Photocopying, desktop publishing systems, print-on-demand, and so forth, have become cheaper and more accessible. Additionally, the proliferation of online media has contributed to the advancement of self-publishing, allowing authors to market themselves, and in some cases to simply publish their work digitally.

The upside of this arrangement for authors is that they have total control and retain all rights. The downside of this arrangement for authors is that they have total control and retain all rights. Self-published authors own their books 100 percent and get all the proceeds of sales—but they also take all the risk.

MIRROR, MIRROR ON THE WALL: VANITY PRESS

The old model of the "vanity press"—a company that publishes books at the author's request and expense—is one well-worn choice when it comes to self-publishing. Vanity press companies contract with authors to package their books regardless of quality or marketability. They appeal to the writer's desire to become a published author, and make the majority of their money from fees for producing the books rather than from sales. In a vanity press arrangement, the author pays all of the cost of publication and undertakes all of the risk. Because vanity presses are not selective, the books they produce are not usually given the same recognition or prestige as commercial publications. And these companies also may charge a higher fee than you'd pay if, for example, you contracted directly with a printer. When published by a vanity press, your book will bear the name and logo of that company. "Vanity publishing" is a loose term; if you go this route you'll need to check with each company to see what services are provided. We discuss some of the variations (i.e. editing, design, etc.) in the following pages.

YOUR OWN HORATIO ALGER STORY: STARTING A PUBLISHING COMPANY

Another model is to start your own publishing company, come up with a name and a logo, and find a book packager and/or printer to work with. This is called self-publishing, or independent publishing, and it is as old as publishing itself. Because of the advances in technology and improved turnaround offered by print-on-demand, this newer model is a growing and increasingly viable choice, at least in some cases. Successful self-publishing requires considerable financial resources and self-discipline.

Tough Love from the Author Enablers

To self-publish means to single-handedly promote your book to the world, using your money, your contacts, your know-how, and your time and energy. It's a daunting task—more daunting, in many ways, than trying to get an agent and a traditional publisher. Self-publishing may or may not be the right choice for you and your book, but we want you to make this decision with your eyes wide open. That's our two cents. ‹ «

THE PRIUS OF PUBLISHING: HYBRID MODELS

There are hybrid models that lie somewhere between self-publishing and vanity presses. Subsidy publishers distribute books under their own imprints, and as a result are selective in deciding which books to publish. Subsidy publishers take payment from the author to print and bind a book, but contribute a portion of the cost as well as additional services such as editing, distribution, warehousing, and marketing, though the quality of these services may be unremarkable and minimal. As with commercial publishers, the books are owned by the publisher and remain in the publisher's possession, with authors receiving royalties for any copies that are sold once the book has earned out. The rights for the book are generally retained by the subsidy publisher and authors have little control over production elements such as cover design.

Print-on-demand (POD) publishers generally do not screen submissions prior to publication. Many POD publishers are web-based, accepting uploaded digital content from anyone who is willing to pay. Authors can design a printing plan that meets their requirements or choose from a selection of packages. For an additional fee, a POD publisher may offer services such as jacket design, editing, proofreading, marketing, and publicity. Some POD publishers are branching into the growing field of e-books, and many offer ISBN (International Standard Book Numbers) service, which allows a title to be searchable and listed for sale.

WHEN SELF-PUBLISHING MAKES SENSE

Self-publishing makes sense for authors who want to have a book published and don't care if it sells at all (e.g., someone who wants to print a family history and give it to every family member and the local library), someone who has a way to sell books independently and doesn't need access to retail book outlets (e.g., a doctor who speaks to hundreds of people many times a year and can sell books at the events; the owner of a bed and breakfast who will sell copies of a history of the building site to people staying there over the years), and corporate entities that are in a position to sell their books directly to a specific audience in enough quantity to justify printing them, even though they won't be distributed in bookstores.

In short, self-publishing is increasingly becoming a viable way to publish. There are a number of reasons for this:

- The POD method has become more affordable with new technology.
- The Internet has become a means for some authors to bypass the traditional publisher/bookstore route—we repeat, *some* authors.
- The Internet and electronic book technology are redefining the very concept of what a book is, as authors can "publish" their books online at almost no cost.

The benefits of self-publishing are:
- Getting a faster turnaround on production
- Keeping your artistic vision intact (in other words, no fights with your editor because you are your editor)
- Receiving significantly greater return on each book sold, without having to wait for unintelligible royalty statements or money held against returns

Rarely, but sometimes, it might even make sense for you to self-publish because you have struck out with the traditional publishing path. Let's say you are a science-fiction writer with a book you believe in, but all the agents and publishers have turned you down. You are a go-getter with resources and time, and you know how to locate sci-fi conventions and review publications. You are savvy enough about marketing to begin with an initial small review mailing that will produce endorsements that you can then include in subsequent larger print runs. Maybe you can break the mold and sell your book yourself. Maybe you can get William Shatner *and*

Leonard Nimoy to give you blurbs, create a sensational website, and perhaps even sell e-books online.

Before you self-publish, there are a couple of questions you should ask yourself: Do I care if my book never gets reviewed in mainstream publications or distributed to bookstores and other traditional book retailers? Do I have enough of a platform to sell this book outside of bookstores without losing my shirt?

THERE'S MORE TO SELF-PUBLISHING THAN WRITING

If you do choose to self-publish you need to know that a lot of hard work will begin after your book is completed. Instead of handing it off and working with your publisher, you'll have to roll into publicity and marketing mode. The first crucial step of any marketing campaign is determining who your audience is. (Some would argue that you should determine this before writing the book.) Next, spend a little money on designing and printing a succinct press release. Then send free copies of your book to any personal media contacts and influential people in your field.

A web presence is a low-cost way of keeping the world informed about any news related to you and/or your book. You can also buy an e-mail contact list from Cision (*www.us.cision.com*) or some other similar service. You probably can't afford a full-page ad in *USA Today*, but you might find another publication, geared specifically to your audience, with reasonable ad rates. Donate books to radio station pledge drives and charity fundraisers. Present yourself as an expert in your field to local and national media outlets. Watch the news, and remind producers that you are available to comment on breaking stories. Always keep a box of books in the trunk of your car, and carry a copy with you when you travel. Network like crazy, but don't be one of those people everyone avoids at parties because you can't talk about anything *but* your book. Once in while, talk to the other guy about *his* book.

The danger of going the self-publishing route is this: no one is great at everything, and it takes an immense amount of resources to publicize, distribute, and market a book. If you aren't out on the lecture circuit and can't afford the time and money it takes to rent booth space at conventions, chances are you're going to end up with a lot of extra product on your hands. It's hard enough to get attention for a new book with traditional publishing resources behind it, so think carefully about whether or not you can sell enough copies to make this worthwhile, without the benefit of media reviews and bookstore distribution.

SUCCESSFUL SELF-PUBLISHING: A TRUE STORY

The following is a personal story from Betty Kamen, a successful self-published author who by a wild coincidence happens to be Kathi's mom!

"My personal success story involves writing and lecturing about a subject that has widespread interest, mainly because it centers on a widespread problem. Women were filling drug prescriptions for relieving the discomfort of PMS (premenstrual symptoms) and menopausal discomfort. I, however, offered a safe and effective natural alternative. So my book had a large audience!

"My major problem with traditional publishing is the loss of control. For example, words I think are essential for a point I am making may be eliminated. And here and there a descriptive expression would be 'dumbed down,' or replaced by one that changes my meaning. A second issue is time—the time it takes to get my book rolling off the printing presses. Why couldn't my publisher see how important it is to put all other projects aside and give MY BOOK priority? These concerns led me to self-publish.

"But first, a warning: I don't think a novice who has never been published professionally should take a stab at self-publishing. You have to earn your right to do that successfully. A major requirement is to know how the professional editors work. It's an excellent idea to sit down with a professional editor to learn how it's done. After such an experience, you now have the potential to self-edit and self-publish. (If you are unpublished, professional editors are available. Check online, or contact your high school English teacher.)

"It's a good idea to give your manuscript to several people for feedback before it goes to press. Offer your work to someone who knows about your subject, to someone who knows nothing about the subject you have explored, to someone who is young, and to another who is old. If your message has been both clear and important, people in each of these categories will come up with almost the same critique, plus unique ideas based on their personal experience and age.

"Then there's the matter of subject. Is your message one that has been previously tackled, again, and yet again? Are you offering a new perspective? Obviously, the latter is essential for success. Make sure your jacket copy and marketing materials communicate to your potential audience that you have something new and important to share.

"Okay, your book is written, and now you have to sell it. If there is any reference to a product in your book, you may want to approach a company that manufactures, distributes, or sells that product. That company may promote your book directly to their clientele, or they may even offer a financial grant, or a percentage of the sales of their product generated as a result of your book. In my case, a company that manufactures a cream that relieves the problem of PMS and menopause (the subjects of my book), bought tens of thousands of copies of my book, using it as promotional material.

"Go through your manuscript with an eye to selecting paragraphs that are provocative. These are excerpts you should be sending to magazines, newspapers, and radio and TV stations, offering yourself as an exciting guest. Broadcasters are always looking for interesting people to interview—yes, even the biggies have staff on the lookout. It's okay to be persistent and follow up. Most importantly, once you are being interviewed, be sure to mention the title of your book and, if possible, contact information for the book's availability. Save the copies of the actual interviews to show to your grandchildren.

"Offering a free lecture in your neighborhood based on your book often produces high sales. Approach the local women's and men's groups, church and synagogue groups, etc. On my very first lecture presentation, a woman came up to me after my presentation, asking for my card. I didn't have a card—but I have never been without one since. I also have a one-page flyer that I leave on every seat before the audience arrives. The flyer contains my contact information, along with a list of my books, and their availability.

"I also start each presentation with a short humorous story. Getting my audience to laugh at the outset assures that they will be attentive. Good luck and good book sales!"

ANOTHER TRUE STORY: PASSION OVERRIDES EXPERIENCE

This self-publishing story was contributed by Emily Scott Pottruck, who decided that self-publishing would be the most effective way to meet her goal, raising money for a good cause:

"I decided that at every decade birthday, I would do something outside of my comfort zone to benefit something that changed my life. Animals entered my life in a big way in my forties, so at fifty I decided to do something that would benefit animal welfare non-profit organizations. I met Amy Tan through my four-legged children (others know them as dogs) and hers, and was exposed to a world of authors and writers.

"Making a long story short, I decided to create a coffee table book that portrayed the bond between people and their pets. It was important to me that all types of households (ethnicities, gender, family structure, etc.) and all types of household pets would be included so anyone with a pet would find someone in the book with whom they could identify. This was not another dog book or cat book. This was a book about the relationship we humans have with our pets.

"I mentioned this to Amy and then with incredible naiveté, I asked her (note: NEVER ask a famous author to do this unless you are either as naive as I was or he/she owes you a huge favor) to write the foreword. Remarkably (which gets more remarkable as I become more learned), she agreed. Thus, *Tails of Devotion, A Look at the Bond Between People and Their Pets*, was born.

"Amy also said, 'If you really want to make money for charity, then you will need to self-publish. There isn't a publisher that would do this for free. Knowing you as I do, nobody will market this as strongly as you will.'

"*Tails of Devotion* would become my birthday gift to myself; I would incur all the costs so *every penny from every sale* would go to charity.

"This is where passion overrides experience. Had I known what I did not know, I would have stopped at this point. Had I known that my desire to have a visually stunning book, well-made, high-quality product would be as costly as it was, I would have written a check to the charities and blown out my birthday candles. Had I known that the process would take 100 percent of my time for sixteen months, then 80 percent for twelve months, then 40 percent for eight months, I would have hired someone and gone to the golf course. The passion I had for *Tails of Devotion* consumed me so I had no choice but to proceed and I am smarter and more fulfilled because of it. I now believe that people are not workaholics but passionaholics. There was nothing I wanted to do that didn't include *Tails of Devotion*.

"In the three years that *Tails of Devotion* has been on the market, almost all 10,000 copies have been sold or distributed, raising more than $250,000 for sixty animal welfare nonprofit organizations in twenty-two states and two countries.

"I benefited from staying true to the mission, which resonated with many experts in the publishing world. Once they learned that I was not recouping my costs, that I was doing my homework, that Amy Tan was writing the foreword, these professionals offered me best practices and their contacts when the questions were outside their field of expertise. A local bookstore chain agreed to fulfill orders from my website for very little compensation. I set up an account at the Schwab Charitable Fund so proceeds could then be distributed as grants. Learning by doing also meant that for every door opened, I not only got more information, but I also entered a hallway of other doors that I had no idea existed that also needed to be opened.

"The biggest obstacle from start to finish (note: especially marketing, public relations, sales) is the perception that self-publishing = vanity press. The assumption is you self-published because every publisher turned you down. As *Tails of Devotion* is a four-color, glossy coffee table book and not the hoped great American novel (note: black ink on paper), I thought this would not be an issue. I was wrong. While I continuously heard from respected publishers that my book was top quality and had all the right marketing ingredients (famous people in the book and as jacket blurbs, artistic and compelling photos, unique structure and selling proposition), many reviewers, TV/radio producers wouldn't even look at *Tails of Devotion* because it was a self-published book."

You may have a similar passion but have been unable to get your book published. If so, Emily has additional suggestions for people considering self-publishing:

- If your work is "black ink on paper" you have many more options for printing. Do use high-quality paper and do invest in an experienced graphic designer to help with cover and layout.
- Distribution, distribution, distribution. Do you really want your office, closet, garage, and kitchen cabinets the only places your book resides? Approach your local bookstores, as many of them have a shelf for local authors. Look into Amazon Advantage, Google Books, gift stores, and other opportunities for consignment. Create a website, blog, and

e-mail list. Approach book clubs, local community centers, cafes, local newspapers, neighborhood newspapers, local radio shows.

- Always carry at least one copy of your book with you—always and everywhere.

- Give away free copies very judiciously. It was amazing how many people—including friends and family—asked for a copy. *Tails of Devotion* proceeds went to charity! Even when I explained this point, people still expected a free copy. The only exception to this is if your objective is to create the book and then give away copies. If that is the case, please send me a copy!

- Expect "yes." *Tails of Devotion* had so many bells and whistles that I truly expected everyone would want to buy the book, would want to interview me, and would want to shower us with glowing reviews. My convictions were so strong that I was truly surprised when I heard "no." Passion overriding experience . . .

- Before you go to press, find at least three people who are staggeringly candid and ask them to review your work and offer comments. Listen to their comments. If all three readers want you to change something, I suggest you take them up on their edit. If the comments are mixed, and you trust your instincts, then go with your gut.

- Once you are done writing and editing, you must then start wearing the hats of marketing rep, distribution/operations manager, and bookkeeper. Or find someone willing to do this for you but stay on top of it. Remember, you care about this book and its success more than anyone else in the world. You are the CEO of your book.

- There are many sites and people offering "how to" and/or promising "success" in all aspects of self-publishing. Be cautious and read the fine print. Much of this information can be found for free on the Internet and in your local public library. Diet pills promise that you can be thin in ten days for the low cost. They don't emphasize the fact that this happens if you eat less and exercise more and that you have now signed up for a monthly plan.

- Create a timeline and a plan of action. Stay focused on the timeline and the plan of action. Then be prepared to constantly redo said timeline and plan of action. The twists and turns cannot be predicted. Challenges and opportunities abound.

At the end of the day be proud of your work, of your effort, of your desire to be creative. These are all wonderful traits!

Famous Books That Were Originally Self-Published Books

Ulysses by James Joyce

Leaves of Grass by Walt Whitman

Walden by Henry David Thoreau

Huckleberry Finn by Mark Twain

Robert's Rules of Order by Henry Martyn Robert

The Tale of Peter Rabbit by Beatrix Potter

The Elements of Style by William Strunk, Jr. and his student E. B. White

The Joy of Cooking by Irma Starkloff Rombauer

The Bridges of Madison County by Robert James Waller

The One-Minute Manager by Ken Blanchard and Spencer Johnson

The Celestine Prophecy by James Redfield

The Christmas Box by Richard Paul Evans

What Color Is Your Parachute? by Richard Nelson Bolles

Legally Blonde by Amanda Brown

The Shack by William P. Young

And, of course . . .
Tails of Devotion by Emily Scott Pottruck
and

Hormone Replacement Therapy: **Yes or No?** by Betty Kamen,
PhD

WHEN SELF-PUBLISHING DOESN'T MAKE SENSE

If you're hoping to appear on major television shows and see your
book on the bestseller lists, self-publishing is not the likeliest route
(although there's no guarantee you will have a bestseller or appear
on TV anyway, even with a title published by A. A. Knopf). But if
you don't care about bookstore distribution and you have a viable
plan for finding your audience, self-publishing can make sense. It
can even be the better choice.

The benefits of working with a publisher are:

- Editorial direction (something most of us actually do need)
- Expert copyediting and proofreading services
- Sales, distribution, marketing, and publicity at a level rarely
  accomplished alone
- Most of the time, a better looking, more salable finished
  product
- The respect among booksellers and media that (as of this
  writing) is conferred only on books published by established
  publishers
- Not having to find space in your garage for the boxes of
  books that don't sell

BOTTOM LINE

Self-publishing can be a great idea for some authors, but it is a lot of work and isn't right for everyone or every type of book. Impatience and frustration aren't the best reasons to self-publish; you need to have resources and a carefully thought-out plan if you are going to go this route. That said, these are changing times, and some self-published authors are finding success by going their own way.

CHAPTER TEN

FOR SALE: BOOKSTORES, BOOKSELLING, AND BOOK GROUPS

In this chapter we will demystify the retail landscape (independent bookstore, chain store, online)—what happens when your book hits the stores, why booksellers are important, what hand-selling means, creative methods for getting the attention of book groups, and why book groups can make a difference. We'll also touch on special markets, co-op promotions, course adoption, and ways to make book signing events unique.

Once your book is written, acquired, and published, and as it is marketed and publicized, the sales team goes to work. This is a two-step process: step one involves the publisher's sales representatives pitching your book as part of the forthcoming list to their accounts (everyone from that tiny bait-and-tackle store with the rack of paperbacks out by the lake to community-oriented independent bookstores, to big chains, to Wal-Mart, to Amazon.com, to phone apps); step two involves the reader walking into (or perhaps Googling) a retail outlet and actually buying your book.

THE CHANGING LANDSCAPE OF RETAIL SALES

Bookselling techniques vary according to the venue, of course. Online sales (a rapidly changing and expanding area) rely on reader reviews, web links, and (in some cases) preferential treatment bought with publisher advertising dollars, such as paying for an arrangement where search engines direct users to a link about the book. Online videos, author interviews, catalogues, book trailers, phone apps, and teasers provided to online retailers or directly to the public are new ways to reach retailers and readers. Others include e-mail campaigns to targeted lists, grassroots networking through social networking sites and websites or blogs with particular interests (nursing mothers, environmental activists, thrill seekers), and authors' websites. However online marketing is done, the goal is the same as it has always been in all book marketing—to promote the book within the industry and to the buying public so that it will capture attention and sell.

BOOKSTORES

There are many different kinds of bookstores, and the ones you visit when promoting your book will be chosen for a variety of reasons:

- The store reports to an influential bestseller list such as the one in the *New York Times*.

- The store specializes in mysteries and you are a mystery writer, or in architectural books and your book is about architecture, etc.
- The bookstore is a leading independent store in your community, hosting well-run events that can help break out a book like yours.
- The publisher has an ongoing relationship with the store.
- The publisher is trying to influence a regional bestseller list by scheduling a lot of events in the same area at the same time.

Chain stores like Barnes & Noble or Borders make their book-buying decisions at a central national office, though local stores often have a display featuring books of local interest or by local authors. An event at these stores can be either a simple book signing or a reading/discussion followed by Q&A and a signing. Make sure you know what is expected of you before you arrive, so you can be professional and prepared.

BIG-BOX STORES

At a warehouse store like Costco or Sam's Club, a limited variety of titles are piled on a table with no apparent thought given to display or promotion. The fact that the books are there at all is an indication of corporate support, but even these stores will host an occasional book signing. If you are asked to sign at one of these stores, expect to field questions from confused shoppers who want to know where to find the electric toothbrushes or small power tools. You might want to brush up on the lay of the land ahead of time, so you can provide the correct answers. Maybe you can make a little money on the side doing a food demonstration! It can be humbling to sit in a warehouse store with a pile of your books and realize they are, in this context, just that much more merchandise. However, having your books stocked by these stores is good news for an author. Warehouse stores order in large quantities and expose your book to an audience that might not ever find it in other retail settings.

INDEPENDENT BOOKSTORES, HAND-SELLING, AND BUZZ

Independent bookstores, or small regional chains, are the most likely venues for "hand-selling," a term you may have heard before. But what does this mean? Hand-selling is the natural extension of that other mysterious term, "bookseller buzz." Here are a couple of examples of hand-selling at its best.

Example #1:

Bookseller: May I help you find something?

Customer: Oh, would you? I need a gift for my great-aunt, and she's very hard to please.

Bookseller: What is she interested in? Do you know what she likes to read?

Customer: Well, she's always knitting something. She's a big believer in conspiracy theories, and there are stacks of *Reader's Digest* magazines in her bathroom, going back to the seventies.

Bookseller: Hmmm . . . how about *The Knit Wit Murders*, by Livinia Smelt? It involves an international spy ring made up of knitters, and the humor is actually similar to that of *Reader's Digest.*

Customer: Why, that looks perfect! Thank you so much.

In this first instance, the bookseller is thinking on her feet, trying to come up with the perfect gift for someone she's never met. Sometimes the bookseller has an ongoing relationship with the customer. They may even be having an affair, but that's none of our business.

Example #2:

Bookseller: Hello, Mrs. Jones, how are you today?

Customer: Just fine, Eloise. What do you have for me this week?

Bookseller: Let's see . . . you read the new Livinia Smelt last week. How did you like it?

Customer: The story was good, but the humor was a little corny for my taste. I think I liked her Doodle Dumpling series better.

Bookseller: Ah! Well then, I have something brand-new for you: *When the Sparrow Cries Wolf*. It's about mayhem and murder in a bird-watching club. I know you and your husband are bird-watchers, and the quirky humor is reminiscent of the Doodle Dumpling series.

Customer: I'll give it a try. You're sure it isn't corny?

Here, the bookseller is working with a regular customer, one whose taste she knows well, and whose past purchases she remembers. This is not the way it works at the big-box stores like Wal-Mart, Costco, etc.

Example #3:

Customer (walking in the door): Hello, how are you today?

Bookseller: Oh, I'm so glad it's you! How have you been?

Customer: Okay. You know, work . . . kids . . . never a dull moment. Read any good books lately? (This is a little private joke, and has been going on for years.)

Bookseller: As a matter of fact, yes! This is hot off the presses, and I think you'll *love* it. I read an advanced reader's copy, and I've been recommending it to everyone—the author is a fresh new voice, with a really creative take on the whole vampire craze. (She hands the customer a copy of Tony's vampire-dog book, *Count Barkula*.)

Customer: Hmmm, I was more in the mood for one of those Middle Eastern romance novels, you know, a classic chador-ripper. But this looks good, too.

In this case, the bookseller has fallen in love with one particular title, and is pushing it to everyone she knows. This is the kind of bookseller who can make all the difference in building an author's career. This is why bookstores, and especially independent ones, matter so much to publishing and why we should support these stores when we can.

INDIEBOUND

An extension of handselling is a consortium of independent bookstores called IndieBound, a group that promotes new books and independent bookstores through various means, including a national listing of recommendations. Books that are selected are often displayed on a special table in the store or with shelf talkers (little cards that describe and endorse the book), and publicists love to tout these selections when drumming up publicity for authors whose books are included.

So, what's the lesson here for a new author? If you've been a good, supportive customer of your neighborhood bookstore (attending author events and buying books in the store, rather than enjoying the free entertainment and then ordering the books for a dollar less online), when your turn as an author rolls around you will already be part of a valuable and important community. The book buyers will know who you are, and will be more likely to order multiple copies of your book. And you'll have at least one bookstore where you'll be able to schedule a reading guaranteed to be well-attended by family, friends, and colleagues. Let's hope they all buy your book!

SPECIAL MARKETS AND GROUP SALES

Another way you, as an author, can influence the distribution of your book is to think of non-bookstore retailers who might be a good fit: museums, music stores, health spas, and tourist attractions often sell a selection of related titles. Even hardware and furniture stores have been known to sell books—any retailer, in fact, who thinks money can be made this way is a potential bookseller. Sales to these retailers are often handled by someone identified as a "special markets" or "special sales" rep.

An area related to special markets is sales to larger groups—for instance, course adoption, when a book becomes part of a school curriculum. This is an essential part of the academic book world and is serious business. Marketing to religious institutions and communities is another large sales opportunity for certain kinds of books.

Kathy Patrick, a force of nature we know in Jefferson, Texas, owns a combination beauty parlor and bookstore, proving that sales need not be limited to bookstores. Beauty and the Book, as you might imagine, caters to the taste of Southern women (every last one of whom is considered by Kathy to be one of her "girlfriends" and *all* of whom have marvelous hair).

Have you written a mystery that takes place at the Grand Ole Opry? The Country Music Hall of Fame has a gift shop. Are you giving a lecture at a health spa? Arrange for your book to be available, even if you have to bring your own copies. Does your subject matter tie into science, or the arts? Museum shops love good books that fit their themes. You get the idea. One way you can help your publisher is to provide ideas and, if possible, contacts, for selling your book outside of traditional bookstores.

Depending on your publisher and the degree of commitment to your title, you might find your book displayed in bookstore windows, on endcaps (displays at the end of rows of shelves), on display tables, or in other preferential locations. This kind of placement is usually paid for as part of the publisher's marketing budget—

and another reason why if you want bookseller attention it can be an uphill battle to self-publish. Independent booksellers are more likely to display books they like and want to support, regardless of what the publishers are pushing, which is another reason why "bookseller buzz" is important.

BOOKSTORE READINGS AND EVENTS

Whether or not you end up going on a full-fledged book tour, you are likely to be asked to do at least a couple of readings in book-stores, so it's a good idea to put a little thought into preparing for these events.

Bookstore events can be structured several ways. For some kinds of books (celebrity biographies, sports stars' memoirs) and events (book signings at publishing conventions and trade shows), only an autographing session is expected. The author sits at a table, usually with someone to help out by opening books to the title page, and simply autographs the books.

Most bookstore events follow this format: reading or discussion, Q&A, and signing. If you're reading, pick a section that is your best performance piece, not necessarily your best writing. You don't have to read from the very beginning of the book, but don't give away any big plot surprises. Our friend Elaine Petrocelli, owner of the wonderful Book Passage stores in the San Francisco Bay Area, tells the story of the mystery writer who came to her store and read the last chapter—yes, the one that gives away the identity of the murderer—to a rapt audience. There were very few books sold that day.

The reading (or talk, if that's more appropriate) section should not be more than twenty minutes long; thirty minutes *tops*. Any more than that, and people will feel like they've already read your book—plus, people get antsy, and some need to go to the bathroom.

How to Sign Your Book like a Pro

Sign the title page. That is the page inside the book that has both the title of the book and the name of the author on it. Ask the person you're signing for if he would like an inscription (for example, "To Maurice"). If the answer is yes, make sure you spell the name correctly. Some people will be thrilled to have a book inscribed, or personalized. Other people prefer just a signature and date. Always ask first.

Some authors like to add a little catch-phrase in addition to their signatures. Maya Angelou writes "Joy!" when she signs books. Matt Groening draws a bunny in each *Life in Hell* book he signs; Kurt Vonnegut used to draw pictures of faces in profile next to his signature; other authors have special rubber stamps made. It's fun to think of a phrase or scribble you can add that's unique to you. Make sure it's something that can be written, stamped, or drawn quickly, though, in case you attract a long line of autograph seekers—a problem we *all* want to have. ‹ «

After the reading segment, you can open the floor for questions from the audience. Many of the people who have come to hear you read will be there because they too want to be published writers, and are hoping that some of your mojo will rub off on them. So be sure to put on your mojo lotion that day. Even if you are the world's foremost expert on flamingo mating habits, you're bound to get questions along the following lines:

- "Do you write longhand, or on a computer?"
- "Do you write every day? What time of day?"
- "Can you send my manuscript to your agent?"
- "Can I date your boyfriend?"

For novelists, all of the above, plus:
- "Is your work autobiographical?"
- "Where do you get your ideas?"

Sometimes you may be tempted to say "None of your business," or "Get a life"—don't. Every questioner is a potential buyer or fan. Be professional, be polite, and keep your cool.

A Bookseller's Two Cents

Kathleen Caldwell owns A Great Good Place for Books in Piedmont, California, a tiny store where big things happen all the time. Here's Kathleen's two cents about why it's important to support your neighborhood bookstore: "I believe independent bookstores represent community. We donate to your child's school auction, we supply books for your fundraisers, we know what you like to read, we host presentations on what your book club should read next, we notice when your child loses a tooth or starts to walk, we ask how your mom is doing, and we're there to support you when you've suffered a personal loss. We live and contribute to your neighborhood—it's important to us that we all thrive." ‹ «

After the Q&A peters out, you'll be led to a special table where a bookstore employee (or your media escort) will help you keep the line of fans moving by "flapping" the books (taking the front flap and placing it so the book opens to the title page) and writing the names to be inscribed on little Post-It notes. If the reading is well-attended and there is a long line, this person will help you be more efficient.

Top-secret tip: you can work out a signal to let your escort or bookseller know if a fan is bothering you. It can be a physical sign, but then you run the risk of scratching an itch on your ear and the next thing you know your favorite auntie is being booted out of the store. We prefer a really stupid-looking pen, one you would never use lightly. Keep it handy but only pick it up if you really mean to communicate the message that "this person is a crazed stalker and I need help," or, more likely, "this person seems to be oblivious to the throng behind her and is making no signs of moving on anytime soon."

If there's a small or nonexistent crowd, you'll want to be charming and chat with the bookseller. Sign some copies for the store and don't forget to say thank you. Although conventional wisdom suggests that signed copies cannot be returned, in many cases this is no longer true—or at least no longer consistent or police-able. However, if you sign extra copies for a bookseller, there is a good chance that an autographed-by-the-author sticker will be slapped on the cover, and the book may even be displayed more prominently.

BOOK GROUPS

Book groups (also called book clubs or reading groups) are becoming an increasingly important part of the publishing landscape. Book groups have been around for a very long time, but have recently become kind of a hot new thing with publishers' marketing departments, who have begun packaging certain books so that they will appeal to these groups. It's not unusual to find group discussion questions (or reading group guides) inserted as appendices to novels. Sometimes local newspapers will coordinate reading groups and provide or suggest titles to read.

Famous book clubs like Oprah's (well, there's nothing really *like* Oprah's except Oprah's) can make a world of difference for an author, and the One City, One Book (or One Book, One City) community reading programs can also make a big difference. Led by libraries or other civic or civic-minded organizations, these programs encourage everyone in the community to read the same book. But even smaller—way smaller—groups can have an effect. The magic ingredient is word of mouth; one group loves a book and spreads the word to friends in other groups, and before you know it you have a national bestseller like *The Red Tent* or *The Kite Runner.* Both of those books caught fire sometime after their original publication, due to book group interest.

TRUE-LIFE ACCOUNTS OF THE IMPORTANCE OF BOOK GROUPS

Kathy Patrick's Pulpwood Queens book club has grown to include hundreds of chapters, mostly in the South and Southeast. Kathy hosts an annual "Girlfriend Weekend" for authors and chapter members in her hometown of Jefferson, Texas—and we know it's a great event because we've been there. Here are a few words from Kathy herself, about the importance of book groups:

"I never knew just how important being a part of a book group was until I started The Pulpwood Queens of East Texas. Six women arrived for that first meeting who were, seriously, virtual strangers. These women grew to be really more than just great friends; they have become my book family. As chapters sprang up all over the country and the world, my world has been expanded beyond my belief. Before I started my book club, The Pulpwood Queens—now the largest 'meeting and discussing' book club in the world—my life's focus was on my family and work, period.

"The difference between life with or without a book club is the difference between cornbread and a sublime and decadent cake. Cornbread is good and sustaining but we want our cake and to eat it too! The fact that new places, cultures, and worlds have opened our eyes to the splendor of our imaginations both on and off the page through our own life's experiences, has made reading as important in our lives as the basic needs of air, water, and shelter. And I haven't even mentioned all the wonderful authors with whom we have met and shared our book club meetings and festivals. The community of shared reading has given us all the tools we need to not only have a productive life but one that is truly valuable, a life that is a true celebration of living."—Kathy L. Patrick, founder of The Pulpwood

Queens Book Clubs and author of *The Pulpwood Queens' Tiara Wearing, Book Sharing Guide to Life*

Ann Kent's Book Group Expo has hosted hundreds of authors and thousands of eager readers and book group members at an annual event in San Jose, California, as well as smaller satellite events all over the San Francisco Bay Area. A successful business-woman, Ann started BGE (*www.bookgroupexpo.com*) because she loved her own book group and wanted to forge a connection with other groups to find out what they were reading. Here's Ann, on the importance of book groups:

"For many, reading is a solitary experience, as is the writing that produced the book that is being read. Poetic justice is served when book groups and authors connect. They need each other. Book clubs and reading groups are all about community and conversation. When authors connect directly—in person, via the telephone, or on a blog—their writing is enriched, and so is the world of books.

"We know the influence of book groups—Amy Tan, Khaled Hosseini, Elizabeth Gilbert, and others will certainly attest to their importance! But an author's connections to book groups aren't just about creating a bestseller. I know that is a great consequence, but the connection is more intrinsic than that. Readers can ask questions about the protagonist. Authors can talk about the characters they've brought to life on the page. It's a conversation. It's a community. And it's one of the many reasons that authors and book groups connecting makes reading—and writing—not such a solitary experience."

Here's another perspective from Susanne Pari, Book Group Expo's program director, and author of a novel, *The Fortune Catcher*.

"Book groups are the perfect environment in which to show off—your house, your crystal, your yappy dogs, your lemon meringue pie, your colorful muumuu, and maybe your husband who still has most of his hair.

"A plethora of recent medical studies show that if you want to live a long good-quality life, social interaction and intellectual stimulation are essential. The first alleviates depression, the second confusion. Ergo, book groups will make you happy and keep you smart.

"Authors, book group members will actually read your work after buying it. (Only about 50 percent of book buyers read the books they buy.) So book group readers are more apt, obviously, to recommend your book to others. And since word-of-mouth is still (see Torah, Bible, and Qoran), the best publicity, reaching out to book group readers should be at the top of your marketing list.

When Book Groups Fall In Love

Every author's dream is to have a book that becomes wildly popular through word of mouth. We are embarrassed to admit that we are hoping that happens with this book. Here are a few examples of very popular titles that reached the "tipping point" because of the special word-of-mouth contagion that can happen when book groups fall in love:

- *The Kite Runner by* Khaled Hosseini
- *The Red Tent* by Anita Diamant
- *The Deep End of the Ocean* by Jacqueline Mitchard
- *Eat, Pray, Love* by Elizabeth Gilbert
- *Water for Elephants* by Sara Gruen
- *The Elegance of the Hedgehog* by Muriel Barbery and Alison Anderson
- *Three Cups of Tea* by Greg Mortenson and David Oliver Relin
- *The Memory Keeper's Daughter* by Kim Edwards
- *The Secret Life of Bees* by Sue Monk Kidd

We need to add a shout out to *The Tipping Point* by Malcolm Gladwell. We don't know that this book was driven by book groups, but it sure did take fire, and of course it popularized the term "tipping point." ‹ ‹‹

"While there are as many different kinds of book groups as there are different kinds of social groups, one uniform characteristic of book group readers is their passion for books. Sure, there are book groups that seem to care more about the dinner or the wine or the gossip than about the literary discussion, but remember that the chosen book is why the get-together is happening at all. And that's because reading—especially reading fiction and non-narrative fiction—is (or becomes) a steady part of these (mostly women's) lives. Whatever happens during the meeting—and often nothing is sacred: arguments, confessions, rants, tears, uncontrollable laughter—it will be that particular month's book that will always be remembered as the catalyst. It's the discussion of a book that gives it the best chance to thrive in the world. Simply, word-of-mouth."

Many bookstores sponsor reading groups and offer discounts to group members. Other groups will only agree to read books that have been published in paperback or are readily available at the public library. There are virtual book groups, national-media book groups, and neighborhood book groups. There are book groups made up primarily of vegetarian bartenders. Some are highly organized endeavors with trained book group leaders; others are as much an excuse to get together, gossip, and drink a lot of wine as they are about reading. There are hundreds of thousands of these reading communities in the United States, most reading one book a month or more. You can see why a reading guide is an important feature in attracting these groups to your book—it enhances the group experience.

Even if a book group is small, it can be worthwhile—not to mention a lot of fun—to set aside some time to visit a few as an author. Writing is a solitary experience, and speaking to these groups can help you to become a better writer, as you meet the audience for your work and make connections with your readers.

BOTTOM LINE

Think creatively about sales opportunities that will work for your unique situation. These days, books sell in a wide variety of venues and locations, and you can work with your publisher to find outlets and opportunities that will enhance your sales.

CHAPTER ELEVEN

LONG LIFE: PAPERBACK AND BACKLIST

Okay, the tour is over, and other books have come along to take up space on the bookstore shelves. When will your book come out in paperback, why is your paperback promoted differently than your hardcover, and what exactly is "backlist," anyway?

You became an author because you wanted to see your name in lights. By now you have probably realized that television and movies might have better lighting, but then, if you are still reading, you are probably a dedicated writer. So—now that you have finished the formal part of promoting your first book, what do you do to keep your writing career going?

EXTENDING YOUR WRITING CAREER BEYOND THE FIRST BOOK

There is no one simple answer to this question, because there are as many paths to a successful writing career as there are authors. For instance, if you are an academic or self-help guru or a religious or business leader, you might want to take some time off from writing to nurture your career and audience (platform), which are the basis of your writing career. But more likely, if your book has been even a modest success, you and your agent will want to strike while the iron is hot to get another book deal. If you are a literary novelist it might take you longer to come up with the next book than, say, a science fiction writer, who may be creating a series and thus already knows the next step.

THE PUBLISHER'S PERSPECTIVE: FRONTLIST AND BACKLIST

One way to think about this is to look at it from the publisher's point of view. Getting out of yourself and understanding this perspective can help you chart your path to success. Broadly speaking, there are two ways a publisher can recoup the initial investment and make money on a book: a book can hit it big when it first comes out—when it is *frontlist*—or sales can grow over time as the book continues to sell without much effort or expense on the publisher's part, when the book is classified as *backlist*. These practices may vary from publisher to publisher, but in general, from a business perspective backlist means that a book isn't part of the current year's budget, whereas frontlist titles are the titles that are being published in the current fiscal year. If, for example, the publisher's budget follows the calendar year, from an accounting perspective a book published November 22 will be frontlist only until the end of the year, becoming backlist in January. The sales people, on the other hand, don't think of a book as backlist for a longer time—generally a year. And when the book is released in paperback, that edition is viewed as frontlist in the same way.

What does this mean for your book? You want your book to succeed (unless you were Emily Dickinson, who was *such* a tease, that little minx). Publishers will keep printing the book as long as there is demand. This means you want your book to stick around long enough to become backlist. However, publishers put the vast majority of their marketing and publicity energy into promoting their frontlist. It's a dilemma. But not really. Publishers love their backlist, which are the books that keep them afloat, and they will buy new books from an author whose backlist is strong and promote both. Think of it this way: backlist titles are the books that succeeded, the ones that sold and are still selling in meaningful quantities. That's why they are still in print. That's why they are backlist.

Practices vary from house to house. Some publishers emphasize selling frontlist and don't do much with the backlist. Others take a longer view and concentrate on backlist. Some do both. Trade publishers need hits that sell big right out of the gate—Is that a mixed metaphor?—but they also appreciate the value of backlist. Smaller publishers—specialty houses and academic presses—have to believe in modest books that will have long lives, because their mission calls for this approach, and because they generally aren't in the business of competing with the big trade houses.

In other words, you don't have to *think* bestseller to get published. You can write a good book, one that a publisher will buy because your editor believes it will have legs and sell year after year. In publishing lingo, this means the editor thinks your book will "backlist." *Moby Dick* has done well in this regard, though we suspect this has something to do with assignments in high school and college English classes. (But we love your work, Mr. Melville! Where do you get your ideas?) Does your book meet the needs of a proven market that is currently underserved? Then it will likely backlist. If you think your book has serious backlist, or long-term, potential, say so in your proposal and back it up with sound reasoning and analysis.

Tough Love from the Author Enablers

As we said earlier, know thyself. Someone said that once, and it's good advice. Don't set out to write a bestseller—set out to write the best book you can. Discover and develop your unique message and voice. Know your field—who has written similar books? Have you read them? You can't be a writer if you don't read, and you can't be an expert if you don't do your homework. ‹ «

Backlist titles that sell year after year generate income for authors and publishers, which is obviously the ideal situation all around. The publisher will use the revenue to buy and promote more books (and pay salaries) and will want to keep you as a "house author." They will want to publish more books by you.

NEW PRESSURES AND TRENDS

In recent years market pressures have forced the large trade publishers to put more emphasis on books that will sell in large numbers right away and to pass over projects that will sell modestly but steadily over the long haul, while smaller publishers have remained open to the latter strategy out of necessity.

The larger houses generally pay larger advances, but the pressure requires them to insist that the author have a strong platform or some other indicator that the book will do well. As a result, the big publishers are less inclined to nurture an unknown or little-known author's career over several books, preferring instead to try and buy established authors or those who appear to have something already going. This means an unknown author may have a better shot with a smaller publisher or an academic press. The big publisher's model is, generally, to push out and sell as many copies as possible, risking returns, over a short span of time. The smaller presses will print fewer copies but will plan on keeping the book in print longer.

BOTTOM LINE

Don't let all this tough business talk scare you. Publishing is an ever-changing industry, but readers still need good books, and your primary focus should be writing one good book at a time. The next steps—agent hunting, proposal writing, and marketing—will be easier to take once you have done what an author is meant to do.

WHAT'S NEXT?

When is it time to stop pushing for that elusive media hit and start writing your next book? Many authors have trouble letting go and moving on. Here's how not to be a one-hit wonder.

While there is no one formula for perpetuating a writing career, we're confident saying this—you need to keep writing. (We warned you at the beginning that we would hammer away at this point. Like the Girl Scouts, the Author Enablers are true to their word.)

"Thank you for that scintillatingly brilliant observation," you sneer, and not without reason. But you'd be surprised at how many people don't realize this—or rather, don't *do* this. Writing is a discipline, and the best approach is to write daily. You will never produce another book (or screenplay or short story or poem) if you don't start. So, put this book down right away and go start writing.

There may be another reason so many people stop writing in a disciplined fashion after that first book—they might be disappointed with the experience. Many books "fail," in the sense that they don't make money, and of those that do make money, few are big hits. The odds of writing a bestseller, especially your first time out, are long. A typical first-time author (or even second- or third-time author) may be discouraged by the experience of being less than an overnight star. It is hard for some of us to accept that we are simply one among many authors. Add to this the fact that your book is likely to have been published by a group of overworked people, some of whom may not have done the best possible job; that you may not have seen your book displayed front and center in stores; that your book may have been reviewed negatively or not at all; and that you may have encountered small turnouts on your book tour (or didn't have a tour at all), and it's no wonder that many authors turn to a new dream that is more easily achieved, such as becoming the first English major in space.

And there is another scenario—fear of success. A first-time author may have had a great run, which can be disconcerting in its own way. There are lots of reasons why someone might be apprehensive after an initial success. Perhaps the author doesn't know if it is possible to follow up with a book that is as good as or better than the first one—in other words, fear of the sophomore slump. Also, most first books are written with the blessing of relative anonymity. There are no expectations and often no deadline—you get to surprise the world with your finished book, and with the fact that you are an author. The second book is a different story. Fans will devour something that took years to write in a few days, then ask for more. Publishers will have ideas about what you should or shouldn't do next. The paparazzi will be camped out on your doorstep, if you happen to live with Brad Pitt. All of this can make it harder to focus on getting the next book written.

Tough Love from the Author Enablers

Everyone's a critic. It's hard, but try not to let negative reviews get to you, and don't let raves swell your head. Neither of these scenarios is good for an author's career. Stayed focused on good ideas and disciplined writing. Remember that you are a writer because you love the written word and have a message or story to share with the world. ‹ ‹‹

Success or not, the real-life experience of getting published can be disturbing for an author for another reason: many writers are introverts, even if they can fake a gregarious nature when called upon to do so. They'd rather be writing or researching than out hustling.

There are more mundane reasons to let your writing go after that first book—you're too darn busy. You have a life, a career, family, friends, pets, your reading to catch up on. You want to go back to school to become a doctor. You believe in the cause you wrote about and want to put your money and time where your mouth is.

Whatever the reason, take our word for it—you *need* to keep writing. You will be mad at yourself later if you stop now, because if you stop now, you will likely not get going again for quite a while, if ever. If you got this far, you have it in you. You are an author now. We don't know if you'll ever have a bestseller or write a world-changing book, but we do know you have something to contribute through the written word.

Give yourself a chance. Most authors don't have a hit with their first book. In fact, a good career can take a number of books to build, with ups and downs along the way. But if you don't write, there is no way for your writing career to grow.

Reboot yourself. Get back to the hopeful and excited frame of mind you were in when you got your first book idea, and let the momentum carry you forward. Remember the simple things: write a little every day; if you use outlines, start a new one; if you need to do research, get to it. Bounce your ideas off a trusted mentor or writing group. By now, you should know what works best for you. Perhaps it's time for you to move out of Brad Pitt's apartment, find someplace a little quieter, and get to work.

BOTTOM LINE

Writing is serious business, but it should also be gratifying and fun—otherwise, what's the point? You know you can do it, and so do we.

Thanks for writing,

KATHI KAMEN GOLDMARK
and SAM BARRY
The Author Enablers

BELOVED BOOKS OF FAMOUS AUTHORS

Some of your favorite authors share their thoughts on the best books to give to the writer in your life—especially if that writer is you. Thanks to the great team at *BookPage* for giving us permission to use some material that has appeared in our monthly column.

THE ART AND CRAFT OF WRITING DEPARTMENT

Amy Tan
Author of *Saving Fish from Drowning*, suggests *Notes on Craft for Young Writers* by John Gardner; all the back issues of interviews with writers in *The Paris Review*; and all the editions of the annual collection *Best American Short Stories*.

Elizabeth Dewberry
Author of *His Lovely Wife*, suggests Robert Olen Butler's *From Where You Dream: The Process of Writing Fiction*. "It's all about approaching the work as an artist, rather than a craftsperson, which is how many teachers approach it. It's about going to that well in you that is your unconscious, or the place where you dream, or maybe even the collective unconscious, but the place where you tap into something much larger than who you are as an individual."

Ridley Pearson
Author of *Killer View*, says *A Writer's Journey* by Chris Vogler should be on every writer's desk.

Kim Addonizio
Author of *Little Beauties*, loves *The Joy of Writing Sex* by Elizabeth Benedict. "This book offers some great ways to get around erotic clichés, like 'a good sex scene doesn't have to be about good sex,'" she says. "There are examples from contemporary writers, useful advice, and, of course, it's an interesting read."

Robert Olen Butler
Author of *Intercourse*, recommends *Aspects of the Novel* by E. M. Forster.

Roy Blount Jr.

Author of *Alphabet Juice*, says, "I know no one wants me to rec ommend the Uncle Remus books, although looking at those pages while my mother read to me from them, when I was little, was formative. Ethno-stereotypical issues aside, Joel Chandler Harris's efforts to spell African-American vernacular (whence springs an enormous amount of American oral and musical culture) was fascinating to me. You could spell things that were real but weren't in the dictionary. There was something almost illicit about it, which was extraordinary coming from my mother, yet also something stone homey. But the main book that has made me a better writer, and now is keeping me from deteriorating too rapidly as a writer, I hope, is the dictionary. The American Heritage one is my favorite."

Anne Lamott

Author of *Plan B: Further Thoughts on Faith*: "I love Lynn Freed's book on writing, *Reading, Writing, and Leaving Home: Life on the Page*. It is brilliant, tough, funny, and incredibly honest, just like Lynn. She's got such a marvelous and dry and sort of nasty sense of humor, and can really make me laugh; but the book is full of wisdom, too."

April Sinclair

Author of *Coffee Will Make You Black*, says that "*Bird by Bird*, by Anne Lamott, is an amazing guide; warm, soulful, funny, smart, honest and instructive . . . *How to Write a Damn Good Novel* by James Frey is the writer's bible when it comes to developing craft . . . *Peaks and Valleys* by Spencer Johnson, MD, both timely and empowering, teaches how to make good times and bad times work for you . . . and Elizabeth Gilbert's *Eat, Pray, Love* is a superbly written, intensely personal, spiritually insightful journey set against the backdrop of three different cultures."

Leslie Levine
Author of *Wish It, Dream It, Do It*, recommends *If You Want to Write: A Book about Art, Independence and Spirit* by Brenda Ueland.

Norman Mailer (1923–2007)
Whose last book was *The Castle in the Forest*: "I confess to being high on *The Spooky Art.*"

Norris Church Mailer
Author of *Cheap Diamonds*, in a random incidence of great minds thinking alike: "My favorite book on writing is *The Spooky Art* by Norman Mailer."

Donna Wares
Editor, *My California: Journeys by Great Writers* and the brains behind *www.californiaauthors.com*: "Carolyn See's *Making a Literary Life: Advice for Writers and Other Dreamers* is inspirational and quirky and a fun read. Carolyn's mantra: 'A thousand words a day, five days a week, for the rest of your life.' I also like *How to Write a Book Proposal* by Michael Larsen. His slim volume is a terrific roadmap for crafting a smart proposal."

Harriet Chessman
Author of *Someone Not Really Her Mother*: "I'd recommend David Huddle's beautifully written book, *The Writing Habit*. I love Huddle's way of couching advice to writers within honest, quiet, cunningly humorous, and always engaging personal essays."

THE JAMES JOYCE FAN CLUB

Scott Turow

Author of *Limitations*, writes: "I'd probably pick James Joyce's *Portrait of the Artist as a Young Man*, not because I learned anything from it I could ever hope to repeat, but because it so perfectly described the passion to write and made me surer of my own desires."

Jane Ganahl

Editor, *Single Woman of a Certain Age*, describes the short story that set her on the writing path: "*Araby* by James Joyce, specifically, this passage about a young boy in love with an older girl—I read it as a junior in college and switched from Political Science to English as a major right then. I still get the chills, reading it again! Haven't we all been there?!"

THE ANNIE DILLARD FAN CLUB

Christine Wicker

Author of *Lily Dale*, suggests "*The Writing Life* by Annie Dillard—beautifully written and minutely observed essays about keeping faith and hope during the torturous process of writing. Two bits of wisdom I think of almost every writing day came from this book. One comes from Dillard's observation of chopping wood. She says that to chop a piece of wood you have to aim through the wood to the chopping block. It's the same with writing. If you aim at the words themselves, they'll have little resonance. You have to strike more forcefully, full heartedly and courageously at the meaning underneath so that the words come tumbling after, flying away in all directions like wood struck with a well aimed ax. The other piece of advice I rejected as absurd and then couldn't stop pondering—like a lot of the best wisdom. She says that you shouldn't write about what interests you most but about what interests only you. That one is difficult, but following it yields all sorts of riches."

Elizabeth Benedict
Author of *The Practice of Deceit: "The Writing Life* is a somber, eloquent meditation on writing that speaks to the difficulties, obsessiveness, and deep pleasures of the process. It also has *the* most useful epigraph, from Goethe, for anyone who does serious work of any kind: 'Do not hurry; do not rest.'"

THE TOM SWIFT FAN CLUB

Dave Barry
Author of *Peter and the Sword of Mercy*, tells us: "A book that helped me write better was *Tom Swift and His Flying Machine.* I read it when I was ten, and I thought: 'This is terrible! I can write better than this!'"

READING FOR INSPIRATION

Stephen King
Author of *Just After Sunset*, checks in with "*The Postman Always Rings Twice* by James M. Cain. He tells a story in 128 pages that many of today's bestselling authors would shoot 500 on. Little tiny sentences, each one a straight punch to the heart. Great book." We'd like to add that we often find ourselves recommending Steve's *On Writing*.

Siddharth Dhanvant Shanghvi

Author of *The Last Song of Dusk*: "Michael Ondaatje's *The English Patient* shimmers with novelistic brilliance: every page is a lesson in the craft of writing and enchantment. It offers innumerable lessons on plotting, the construction of sentences, the blending of poetry and prose, and it sings with a deep and glistening sorrow."

Jonathan Kirsch

Author of *The Grand Inquisitor's Manual*, is inspired by "*The Slave* by Isaac Bashevis Singer. *Any* book by IBS will teach important lessons to a writer about both the craft of writing and the way a writer needs to use his or her head, heart and eye. Singer's collected stories (newly reissued by the Library of America) offer a wealth of inspiration and instruction. But *The Slave* remains my favorite."

Lynn Freed

Author of *Reading, Writing & Leaving Home: Life on the Page*, finds that "reading the letters and diaries of great writers can be, if not always inspiring, of some comfort. For instance, Franz Kafka diaries contain the following entry: 'January 19, 1914: Great antipathy to *Metamorphosis*. Unreadable ending. Imperfect almost to the foundation. It would have turned out much better if I had not been interrupted at the time by the business trip.'" (*The Diaries of Franz Kafka*, 1914–1923, translated by Martin Greenberg with the cooperation of Hannah Arendt, New York: Schocken Books, 1949, p. 12)

Jacqueline Mitchard

Author of *All We Know of Heaven*, tells us: "I found *The Birth House* by Ami McKay on a bench in an airport. What a lucky day for me. I nearly missed my plane as I fell head first into this unsparing, emotionally rich but not a bit sentimental story of a young girl who befriends an elderly midwife who claims to have chosen Dora at birth to be the next practitioner of her obsolete art. It was enthralling, transcending any genre, and a darned good story, too."

Lalita Tademy
Author of *Cane River* and *Red River*: "If you've ever wondered how dramatically altered a life could be by making a single momentary choice, read *The Post Birthday World* by Lionel Shriver. With fierce insight and complex, nuanced characters, Shriver tells Irina's story (hinging on whether or not she kisses a man to whom she is attracted) in alternating chapters of reality unfolding in different directions."

Diana Abu-Jaber
Author of *Origin*: "Writing a thriller gave me a new appreciation for the form. Among the many wonderful models I turned to, Kate Atkinson's *Case Histories* was a real standout—a fine confabulation of intrigue and character—one of the most 'literary' mysteries I've had the pleasure of reading."

David Leavitt
Author of *The Indian Clerk*, adores Jane Gardam's *Old Filth*. "She tells the story of a 'Raj Orphan'—born in Malaysia to a British Colonial bureaucrat at the turn of the twentieth century and then shipped back to England to be educated—and his uneasy adjustment to a world radically different from any he has known. The hero becomes a famous barrister in Hong Kong known affectionately as 'Filth' (Failed in London, Try Hong Kong). An engaging, funny, and moving novel."

Catherine Brady

Author of *The Mechanics of Falling and Other Stories*, loves:

"Marilynne Robinson, *Gilead*. The novel is told in the form of a letter from an aging preacher to his young son; the preacher anticipates he'll die before his son comes of age and wants to leave this letter for him. Well written and deeply spiritual, the novel achieves a rare thing in creating a convincingly good man in its narrator and making you share his faith in life. *The Selected Letters of Anton Chekhov*. There was once a cartoon in the *New Yorker* with one mechanic, working under a car, peering up at his fellow mechanic to say, 'And, of course, Chekhov.' He's such a perfect short story writer, and his letters are embedded with gems of wisdom, not just about craft but about the honesty a writer must cultivate."

Harriet Chessman

Author of *Someone Not Really Her Mother*: "One inspiring book is simply a book of poetry by Mark Doty, *Atlantis* . . . I have found great inspiration in the honesty and heft, sharpness, and beauty of his poetic voice. Even though I write fiction, his poetry (which has a beautiful narrative angle, often) inspires me to listen to my best and most fertile writing self. Virginia Woolf's essays in *The Common Reader* and other books are also wonderfully inspiring to me."

Andrew Sean Greer

Author of *The Confessions of Max Tivoli* and *The Story of a Marriage*: "Honestly, I never know what will inspire other writers except work that seems aesthetically related to what they're working on. I love *War and Peace*, so I'll give them that, and figure at some point in their lives they will open it and read it and find something that works for them. But I would never expect a writer to read anything except what works for them at the moment. The best we can do is to introduce them to surprises that may inspire: for instance, Richard Hughes, *A High Wind in Jamaica.*"

SOME AUTHORS' FAVORITE BOOKS TO GIVE AS GIFTS

Ben Fong-Torres
Author of *Becoming Almost Famous*, likes to give *Elvis at 21: New York to Memphis* by Alfred Wertheimer. "Elvis fans, get ready to get all shook up. Wertheimer got a job shooting publicity photos for various, mostly boring recording artists in the Fifties. Then along came Elvis, and along with him went Alfred—on the road, into dressing rooms, shooting TV rehearsals, in the recording studio, on stage, and, most deliciously, off stage, canoodling with female fans at coffee shops or in a corridor, sneaking a kiss. A stunning volume."

John Lescroart
Author of *Betrayal*, loves *Turpentine* by Spring Warren: "Spring is tremendously talented and this book has utterly captivated everyone who's read it. A great present—enjoy!"

Leonard Maltin
Author of *Leonard Maltin's Movie Guides*: "*Memories of a Munchkin* by and about Meinhard Raabe, the Coroner of Munchkinland in *The Wizard of Oz*. Daniel Kinske has surrounded Raabe's amazing personal memorabilia with a wealth of other Oz-related material, and commissioned a number of great artists (including the late Al Hirschfeld) to provide interpretations of Raabe's famous scene in the classic film."

Sara Davidson, author of *Leap!*: "For spiritual inspiration, I'd give *Your Soul's Compass* by Joan Borysenko and Gordon Dveirin."

Luis Urrea

Author of *The Hummingbird's Daughter*, loves "Jack Kerouac's original scroll version of *On the Road*, amazing for fans and road maniacs, with all the bad language, real names, and naughty bits restored—and the new Library of America's edition of Jack's road books."

Crystal Zevon

Author of *I'll Sleep When I'm Dead: The Dirty Life and Times of Warren Zevon*: "My all-time favorite is *Stories of God* by Rainer Maria Rilke; but this year I'm recommending the beautifully written and thought-provoking novel *Shantaram* by Gregory David Roberts."

Rabih Alameddine

Author of *The Hakawati*, says "I don't particularly care for inspirational books or how-to books, especially when it comes to writing. What inspired me to write were novels. I could name quite a few, but the top of the list, the one that I would give to anyone who wishes to write is Italo Calvino's *If on a Winter's Night a Traveler*. It's about reading, writing, and enjoying the entire lunatic world of fiction."

Daniel Handler, AKA Lemony Snickett

Author of *The Latke Who Couldn't Stop Screaming: A Christmas Story*, illustrated by **Lisa Brown**: "Lately I've been giving people I love a book I love by Joshua Beckman entitled *Your Time Has Come*. It's a striking, tiny book full of striking, tiny poems, perfect for all the striking people in your life, whether or not they are tiny and whether or not they like poetry."

Janis Cooke Newman
Author of *Mary Todd Lincoln*: "Everybody with a kitchen should own a copy of *Joy of Cooking* by Irma S. Rombauer and Marion Rombauer Becker. The 1975 edition is the best, acknowledging the invention of the microwave and including advice on how to prepare opossum."

THE ROCK BOTTOM REMAINDERS' FAVORITE BOOKS TO GIVE TO CHILDREN

Dave Barry, lead guitar
Coauthor of *Science Fair*: "For girls, I highly recommend the 'Doll People' series by Ann Martin, Laura Godwin, and Brian Selznick. These three books—*The Doll People*, *The Meanest Doll in the World*, and *The Runaway Dolls*—are wonderfully imaginative and have great page-turner plots. I read the first two to my daughter, Sophie, who would not let me stop reading; she devoured the third on her own. For younger readers, you can't beat the 'Pigeon' books by Mo Willems, which are hilarious and a little weird, not unlike Mo Willems himself."

Roy Blount Jr., background vocals
Author of *Alphabet Juice*: "*Mrs. Discombobulous* by Margaret Mahy, illustrated by Jan Brychta. The eponymous Mrs. D. is always all up in her husband's face—she calls him, among other things, 'Mr. Tom Fool Noodle'—but then she falls into the washing machine, and after due consideration—'Swish swash do the wash, swish swash do the wash'—he saves her. She is moved to think about the way she has been talking to him and she promises to be nicer. That's the bare bones, which are fleshed out by lots of colorful vituperation from the Mrs., which my kids loved to hear and to repeat, and which

I loved to read aloud. As I recall, the washing machine also goes 'Frooom.'"

James McBride, saxophone
Author of *Song Yet Sung*: "I liked Beverly Cleary's books on Homer Price when I was a kid because I always wanted my own bicycle. That took years to happen, and by the time I got a bicycle I was so old I didn't like her books any more."

Amy Tan, rhythm dominatrix
Author of *Saving Fish from Drowning*: "*The Little Prince*. It's a book for all ages, and at all ages we experience moments of loss and also become lost. The Little Prince is able to find what matters by looking beyond assumptions. He reminds us to not limit our hope to what we assume is 'realistic.' He thinks you can still find what most think is forever gone. It's a good book to read when you are becoming cynical about the world—in other words, a book for many to read now."

THE LIFE CYCLE OF A BOOK

What happens to your great idea between the moment of conception and the remainder bin? Oh! Uh, actually we meant the *New York Times* bestseller list. Here's an overview of the many mysterious stages of publication.

WRITING

We said it at the begining of this book and we'll say it again—the writing comes first. There is no one way to complete a manuscript, but the most important thing is to sit down and get started. So if you haven't written today, stop reading this now and write two pages. Then come back and keep reading.

It's a good idea (but perhaps not essential) to have some sense of what you want to accomplish when you begin, but remain open to changing course if the writing leads you that way. Maybe your family saga about eighteenth-century Czech cheesemakers just doesn't work in the first person (from the point of view of the soup ladle) and wants to be in the third person. Maybe your characters will let you know what they want to do; maybe you'll get to boss them around. Perhaps your sweeping history of civilization viewed through the lens of nap taking has morphed into a more focused look at bed making—be open to the possibility that the new direction may be the one you should follow and that you may have more than one book idea going simultaneously. Some authors like to write detailed outlines and character studies, while others like to be surprised as the manuscript unfolds. Perhaps your historical treatise requires years of research. By all means max out that library card. But while you're at it, don't forget to write, and don't be afraid of where the writing takes you.

MORE WRITING

Once you've completed a first draft, you'll need to reread your manuscript with a sharp eye out for all manifestations of weakness: redundancies, inconsistencies, and inaccuracies. We recommend reading out loud, even if it's just to the dog or the goldfish (or both). Once you've corrected glaring errors, find a trusted friend or two (aside from the dog) to read your manuscript. It's best if you avoid asking people with personal agendas—your doting grandmother, let's say, or your ex-husband. You'll want the opinion of intelligent people who love to read, and who aren't afraid to give constructive criticism. Give your readers plenty of time, remembering that most people are too busy to concentrate on your writing above all else—and never give anyone the only copy of your manuscript. This might also be a great time to join (or start) a writers' group or enroll in a creative writing class at your local college or library, where you'll be able to get feedback on your own writing while reading and critiquing others'.

Tough Love from the Author Enablers

You know who you are—you say you're a writer, but no one's ever seen your work. What—you think you're a shy version of J. D. Salinger? Find a writing companion, writers' group, or class. Not later—do it now! ‹ «

AGENT SEARCH

Once your manuscript is in very good shape, the next step is finding a literary agent to represent you. Publishers generally look more seriously at projects that are represented by literary agents, especially if the author is relatively unknown, and that's only one reason why it makes sense to have an agent. Agents know the editors and how to pitch to them. They can set deadlines for responses to a proposal, identify problems in your contract that you might not notice, and act as your designated nagger when you need information from your publisher, allowing you to be the sweetheart in kind of a good cop/bad cop scenario. Agents usually have specialties, and a good place to start looking for the right one for you is a publication called *Literary Market Place*, available in libraries and online at *www.literarymarketplace.com*. LMP features a listing of reputable agents with a brief description of each one's focus.

You can also meet agents at most writers' conferences. There are good conferences all over the country, and many offer opportunities to help out as a volunteer if you can't afford the tuition.

Yeah, yeah . . . we know all this can be a frustrating and time-consuming process. It's a little like being told that you can't get a certain job until you have five year's experience in the field, and you can't get the experience without getting the job. All we can say is if you want to be published, then it's worth hanging in there. It'll be well worth the time and effort—and the frustration—once you find the right agent to champion your book.

Everyone Needs An Editor

It is possible to get published without an agent, and for that matter, without a publisher. If you decide to represent yourself to publishers, we suggest you hire a professional editor/copy-editor to look over your work. ‹ ‹‹

MORE WRITING

Guess what? Even if an agent loves your manuscript and wants to represent you, chances are you will be asked to make some changes. So batten down the hatches and get ready to do another rewrite.

ACQUISITION

You do your rewrite and the agent LOVES your book. Then what? While your manuscript is being shopped around to publishers, you'll be best off trying to distract yourself with just about anything else you can think of. Go ahead, wax that kitchen floor! Get a pedicure! Take up chess! Read a good book! Start writing another book! Nagging your agent won't help—you just have to trust the process. The process can be a long and anxious one, until the magic day when your phone rings and your agent delivers the news that there's an offer for your book.

Sometimes, if there's more than one offer on the table, a book will go to auction. This means that several publishers are interested and willing to bid on the right to publish your book. But usually—honestly—first-time authors are likely to feel lucky if one publisher makes an offer. Be prepared for a few more weeks of nail-biting while your agent negotiates the details of your contract, and then . . .

GUESS WHAT? MORE WRITING!

Once the contract is signed, you'll begin your professional relationship with your in-house editor, who will carefully read your manuscript and give you notes for—you got it—yet another rewrite. This is the beginning of the part of the process when your book is no longer totally your own, but heading toward being the result of the hard work and effort of (you want to hope) a crackerjack team of pros.

EDITING

In the best of all possible worlds, you will have a great deal of respect and admiration for your editor, who in turn will have a great deal of respect and admiration for you. You'll work together with the same goal in mind—making your book as good as it can possibly be. You'll listen to each others' suggestions with open ears, choose your battles when disagreements arise, and carefully consider all editorial notes. Let's assume this relationship is functioning properly. Once you get notes from your editor, do your best to follow them as you work on this rewrite. Make every effort to get your rewrite finished by the deadline, because a lot of other factors—many of which you've probably never thought about—are riding on the manuscript being completed by a certain date.

While everyone's writing and editing away, a lot will be happening behind the scenes at your publisher's office.

PRE-PUBLICATION

In the six months leading up to the publication date, your focus shifts away from writing and on to many new areas, such as:

GALLEYS

Galleys (sometimes called AREs—for advance readers editions or ARCs for advance readers copies) look like paperback versions of your book with a lot of typos in them. This is because galleys are printed before final copyediting is completed. Galleys (or AREs or ARCs) are used for several purposes. They are sent to book reviewers and other media, especially those requiring a long lead-time for reviews or interview booking. They are also distributed to book buyers at retail outlets and others who can influence advance orders. When you hear about "early buzz" for a title, this usually means that booksellers have read the galleys and are excited about the forthcoming book. It's a good thing. Also, they are often used for soliciting endorsements.

CATALOGUE

Not unlike the catalogues you get in the mail at holiday time, this is an in-house publication used by the sales and publicity team. Your catalogue page will typically have an image of the cover (though this, and even the title, may change before publication rolls around), a description of the book, an overview of the publicity and marketing plan, and a bit of information about you. It's important, for example, for booksellers and media outlets to know where you live and work, so they'll know how flexible your time will be when it comes to booking interviews and appearances. If you have a website, it might be mentioned here, and your previous publications and media appearances may be included. The catalogue is seen by librarians, book and gift buyers, university professors, other publishers, and—who knows—maybe even an enterprising movie producer or two. The decision to catalogue your book means that the publisher has made a fairly firm decision about a number of aspects of your book, such as the title, subtitle (for nonfiction), price, and publication date. Timing is based on many factors, including the state of your manuscript, the business needs of the publisher, and your writing and genre. In the world of bookselling, each season has its own personality, and you'll be listed in the appropriate catalogue. There are many, many exceptions, but "big" books are usually released in the fall, gift and self-help in the winter, and lighter reading in the spring/summer seasons. We say there are many exceptions because there really are—a publisher might release a big fiction title in the summer because the manuscript was delayed or the style of book lends itself to that season. An important book about some great historical figure might be tied to the birth or death anniversary or some other important life event. Religious holidays, Mother's Day, Father's Day, elections, and so on are all considered when a book's timing is being determined.

As with so many other areas, ever-changing technology is influencing these mechanisms. Catalogues are going online, making the seasonal distinctions less important. But much remains the same; books are still timed to coincide with the appropriate season of the year, and once a book is announced to the world in the catalogue, a publisher is usually committed to its publication.

INTERIOR DESIGN

In publishing, interior design includes front matter (the title page, Library of Congress page), typesetting, page layout, photos, illustrations, and dingbats (those ornaments, characters, or spacers that you see in typeset documents, also known as a printer's ornaments or characters). Interior design is often done by a professional designer and is overseen by the managing editor, the behind-the-scenes person who coordinates the publisher's editorial activities.

YOUR BOOK JACKET

Your book jacket (or cover, if your book is released in paperback) consists of some or all of the following: the art, the copy, your author photo and bio, and endorsements (often called "blurbs"). Covers matter, but they are controlled, to a large extent, by the publisher. There may be several designs considered for the cover art, and you will most likely be asked to provide your own author photo. Most first-time authors must waive the right to cover approval. This actually makes some sense, since publishers are more experienced at knowing what will go over with a particular market—and frankly, they are also a little more objective. You'll be able to express your opinion, but at some point you'll have to allow the professional people on your team to do their job.

Cull your address book for people who will endorse your book. We do not think you should ever be rude or unable to take no for an answer when asking a favor of someone, but we also want to stress that this is not a time to be shy. Anyone you know (or whom someone you know knows) and who makes sense as an endorser is worth approaching. This includes prominent writers, of course, but depending on the nature of your book, it can also be respected leaders, experts, and even clowns, if your book happens to be about the House of Representatives . . . or the circus. It all depends on the book. Anyone you know in media, from the high and mighty to the local, can be helpful.

A Little More about Blurbs from our *BookPage* Column

There are several ways to go about getting endorsements from fellow authors, but it almost always helps if you have some kind of personal connection. Like most of us, authors get a kick out of reading their friends' books, and many are honored to be asked to provide endorsements for people—and work—that they love. So where does that put the first-timer with no fancy connections? You'll have to work harder, with longer lead-time built in, to get the blurbs of your dreams.

Unless you have a Rolodex filled with personal friends who are bestselling authors, at most publishing companies it's the editor who gets endorsements, usually starting with other authors in her stable, seeking endorsements from those whose books are similar to yours. For example, as exciting as it might be to get a quote from famous children's author Tomie dePaola, your editor wouldn't seek him out to endorse a psychological thriller about vampire dogs. By sticking solidly within your genre, the editor sees to it that the endorsements provide a helpful marketing tool meant to attract potential buyers.

If your publisher is unable to seek endorsements on your behalf, then it's up to you. This is where writers who make a point of becoming part of their local literary communities have an advantage. Is there an independent bookstore hosting regular events and book signings? Go. Meet people. Get to know the owners. Don't be a pest, but let people know you are about to have a book published. Is there a writers' conference nearby? Go. Meet people. It won't happen overnight, but after a while you'll find that you are part of a thriving community of readers and writers—and you'll have met some established authors. Many cities have active chapters of organizations like the Women's National Book Association, groups that provide regular gatherings and networking opportunities. Go. Meet people.

You can also send out galleys with polite requests for endorsements. Write to the authors in care of their publishers and allow plenty of lead time. Don't take it hard if an author says no—many have a policy of not reading other people's work when they are writing—but it's also possible that you'll catch someone at just the right time, and with just the right captivating manuscript, to get that endorsement. ❮ ❮❮

BIG-MOUTH LISTS AND GIVEAWAYS

Don't overdo this, but there are times when it makes sense to give a book away because it atracts attention or provides some goodwill. This is similar to your endorsement list, except you don't need to know these folks as well—after all, you are giving them something for free. But you don't want to ship your precious books out to be tossed aside, so lay some groundwork—make contact with the people in the media, and prominent figures (or their assistants) to whom you intend to mail the book. Find out where and when it is best to send the package. If you don't hear back, follow up after an appropriate amount of time. If you still don't hear back, perhaps it's time to move on.

DEVELOP AN E-MAIL LIST

While you're developing your short list of endorsers and your big-mouth list, you should also start building a bigger e-mail list of people to notify when you are doing events and when your book is released. Again, this is no time to be shy, and the only rule is to avoid being rude. These are the Wild West days of online communities, with Facebook, MySpace, YouTube, Fwix, blogging, twittering, skittering, and blittering being all the rage. Even as we write this the possibilities for marketing yourself online are evolving and changing, so we aren't going to pretend that there is one way and we know what it is. We do know that this is a real and potentially effective way to get the word out, so at the very least you need to develop an e-mail/contact list and have a decent website. It's possible that your publishing team may develop a website for you, but even if they do, the content on yours will help them get it right.

CLAIM YOUR EXPERT STATUS

In case you didn't realize this, as an author you are an expert, and you need to get used to the idea. This is especially true for nonfiction writers. If you've written a book about aardvarks and their wily ways, get the word out to media that you are the "go to" person on the aardvark issues of our day. Why does this matter? If you present yourself as an expert you may well be called upon by media to comment on your area of expertise, leading to interviews, speaking engagements, and free publicity. If you are a novelist, then you are an expert on everything. Well, maybe not quite, but you are an expert on writing fiction, and if you write in a certain genre you are an expert in that: a time and place if you write historical fiction, crime if you write mysteries or thrillers, horror if you write horror, and so on.

CREATE YOUR DREAM INTERVIEW

It is a good idea to come up with ten good interview questions and ten good book club or reader's guide questions to give to your publicist. Start by imagining your dream interview and write it down. (Oprah was weeping as she alternately hugged me and then my book. "I love your book," she cried, holding it aloft as if it were the Holy Grail. "Please tell me more about You!") You can look online for author Q&As and reading guides if you are unsure how to do this. Generally these are designed to pique interest in the book by drawing the reader in without giving away the farm.

REALITY CHECK

Nobody's perfect, and stuff happens. Remember to be courteous to the people on your marketing and publicity team, even when they make mistakes. These publishing professionals are generally overworked and underpaid, and you will not get more out of them by making them feel bad. A better way to motivate them to higher heights is by doing a good job yourself and by being encouraging, creative, and cooperative.

PUBLICATION PERIOD

Although many new authors expect a book tour to be part of the deal, fewer authors are sent on tour these days. Tours are expensive, and it's difficult to quantify their effectiveness. Instead, many publishers rely more heavily on the "tie-in tour," a fancy way of saying that they'll help you drum up some interest if you happen to be traveling on your own dime. Obviously, lead time is needed—don't expect to be able to tell your publicist that you're flying to Portland on business next Tuesday, so can she please arrange a bookstore signing and a full day of media interviews? But if you know, one to two months in advance, that you'll be somewhere on the publisher's radar, be sure to tell the right people.

Should you happen to be one of the lucky authors who is sent on tour, see our handy survival tips on pages 117–120. But if you're not touring, there are still a lot of ways to get the word out about you and your book.

YOUR MARKETING AND PUBLICITY TEAM

Whether your publisher is a small independent or one of the big conglomerates, the people who work in publishing are, by and large, dedicated professionals who love books. They wouldn't be in this business if they weren't book lovers—publishing is generally not the most lucrative career. In fact, publishing pays less than most other white-collar jobs, and less than many jobs in other media. Yet the pressure to produce results can be at least as intense.

These dedicated folks work long hours juggling several titles at once, trying to figure out how to get the word out about their books (one of which is *your* book) in a market where many competitive titles and distractions clamor for readers' attention. That's why a box of chocolates from the author, arriving at the office mid-afternoon, can help you by perking up spirits and earns you the lasting loyalty of these hard-working pros out of all proportion to the cost of the gift. While you're at it, get yourself some chocolate. You deserve it, too. And how about your sweetheart?

MOM, DAD, AND SIS

Tastefully and respectfully let your family, friends, and various local circles of people know you've written a book. Of course you're going to give some of the closest folks a copy—that is, if it isn't an exposé of your family's foibles. But don't get carried away. Your family, friends, and colleagues can help get sales off to a running start. Resist the temptation to give a free copy to everyone you know. You need the people who love you (or even just like you) to *buy* your book. Let your people support you in this project if they possibly can, because every single sale encourages a bookstore to order another copy from your publisher. And that's what you want (and, whether they know it or not, what your family and friends want for you)—recorded sales.

YOU ARE THE GREATEST

How often have you heard an author say, "Oh, it's not really literature but it was a fun bit of a romp to write" or "I wish I'd had one more crack at a rewrite" or "I'm not really a writer; this all happened by accident." Doesn't that make you want to stuff a wet sock in that person's mouth?

Never put yourself or your book down (metaphorically speaking—you don't have to bring it into the shower with you). Think about it—if you are down on yourself and your book, why should someone else plunk down the cash and spend hours reading your writing? It's good to be charmingly humble and employ graciousness and good manners at all times, but it's also important to be confident and take pride in your work. If you are not ready to promote yourself and your writing, maybe you're not ready to become an author.

SOME REAL THINGS YOU CAN DO TO HELP

Visit local bookstores. Booksellers can make a difference for unknown and emerging writers. Many stores host author events and are an important part of their communities' cultural landscape as well as the American book scene, and even the smallest store can help to shape the tastes and reading patterns of its customers. Sometimes we forget that human culture is still very much a word-of-mouth affair, even if that word-of-mouth is being delivered on Facebook or via text message. Books are often sold one by one (this is called hand-selling), when a trusted bookstore employee mentions a title to a customer at just the right time. So make friends with the smart, dedicated, hardworking people who work in your local bookstores. Introduce yourself and let them know you are an author. Don't pester them about placement of your book or sales—just let them know you are published, what your book is about, and that you are available for events—or to introduce other authors at *their* events. Think long haul, here—if a store can't do an event for your first book, maybe you can ask again for your paperback reprint, or for your next book.

How to Be a Hero to Booksellers

Elaine Petrocelli, owner of Book Passage in Corte Madera, California, shares her tips for getting on her good side.

"Get to know your local independent booksellers—and please, don't wait until your book is published. Recently a publisher called to tell me about a book she was about to bring out. When she said, 'By the way, the author wrote a large part of her book in your café,' I couldn't wait to read it.

Go to lots of author events at your local store and do buy the speakers' books. As you are purchasing, be sure to let the staff know that you love the store and that you are working on a book. If the store offers writing classes or writing conferences, sign up. Don't be pushy. Booksellers get pushed a lot, and they love people who are appreciative and understanding. A few years ago I was in my office working madly to meet our newsletter deadline. A colleague called me to say, 'A woman named Linda is here and she says she needs to see you.' As I came out to meet her, I wondered what the problem might be. What I found was a beaming woman with a bottle of champagne and several glasses. She said, 'My husband, Sheldon Siegel, took a mystery writing class here.

He attended your Mystery Writers' Conference last summer, and now he's in a critique group with several writers he met here. He just got a three-book contract. We want to celebrate with you and our friends at Book Passage.' Believe me, this author's books are always prominently displayed in both our stores. He's now the co-chair of our Mystery Conference. We love having events for his books and the booksellers at Book Passage consider him our own" ‹ ‹‹

Speaking of bookstore events, when you do get to do one, be a pro. Think of ways to make your presentation fun and interesting. An author we know named Lynne Hinton wrote a novel called *Friendship Cake* about a group of women writing a church cookbook, and her publisher sponsored bakeoffs in every bookstore at which she appeared by providing a gift-basket prize for the customer who brought in the best homemade cake. It may sound hokey, but these events drew crowds with the irresistible guarantee of yummy refreshments at all of Lynne's readings. Now, if your book is a thriller about FBI agents chasing a serial killer or a nonfiction book about the role of insects in shaping life in North America, then the bakeoff idea won't work, and you're just going to have to come up with another idea (maybe a g-string for G-men or an "ants in your pants" dance?).

Whether or not gimmicks are your style, it's important to be an engaging and professional reader—a true performer. Here are some essential tips:

- Choose your reading section wisely and run it by a trusted advisor. Print it out in large-point font so you don't have to squint or fumble for your glasses.
- Don't rely on using a copy of your book from the bookstore shelves; it can be hard to read in certain lighting—and if the worst happens and the bookstore order hasn't arrived before your event, you'll still be able to do your shtick. Also, it always

looks a little silly when authors spend time stumbling around their own books, looking for the part they intend to read.

- Make it a short reading—twenty minutes will do. Rehearse several times over several days.

- Remember to show up on time, sober and looking good, unless you are Hunter Thompson or Dylan Thomas, both of whom are dead.

- Whatever you do, always be nice to people—both the public and the bookstore employees. As we said before, books are sold one person at a time. Every fan you make can introduce other fans to your work. If no one shows up, you can still forge a relationship with the bookstore employees—who, we noted earlier, are the people who hand-sell books to the public.

Enjoy The Ride

Finally—and we really really mean this—take care of yourself. Take care of the people you love. Eat right, pay the bills, and keep breathing. Maintain your sense of humor. See a movie. Take your aardvark for a walk. Remember, there's more to life than your book.

Publishing, like much in life, is a crapshoot—you could have a great book that releases the same day as some epic news event, and there goes your media opportunity. Or you could have a quiet book that no one, even you, expects much from, but it captures the zeitgeist (whatever that is) and takes off. Stay balanced and keep the faith. ‹ «

Always let your publicist know if you can get a piece published in a magazine, newspaper, or online, or if you arrange any media or bookstore events on your own. Communicating with your publicity and marketing team will help them to help you. If you arrange an important media appearance without letting them know it may actually cause problems—they may not be able to book you something better because that outlet will feel that the story has already been told. Timing is also important—even big-time authors can blow their publicity opportunities by appearing on air months before a book is released. If *Fresh Air* has you on in January, they're not going to have you on again in September just because your book is hitting the stores. Remember—this is a marketing and publicity campaign, and it calls for strategic thinking and teamwork—not impulsive behavior and ego.

ROLLING INTO BACKLIST

When your book first comes out it is considered "frontlist," which, as we said earlier, is a term that refers to the publisher's list of new or current titles. Although the terminology and accounting practices may vary from publisher to publisher and book to book, a general rule of thumb is that a book is frontlist for a year. If it is released in hardcover, a common practice is to release it in a paperback edition a year later to reach a different group of readers. (Often the hardcover goes out of print at this point.) The paperback edition is also considered frontlist. A year after that release the book becomes a backlist title.

The reason for the designation is more than just a matter of accounting: a strong backlist is generally seen as the way for a publisher to be profitable. Frontlist titles cost the publisher money, and many never earn back what it cost to pay the author, produce, market, and publicize the book. The costs for backlist are much lower, being mostly a matter of printing, warehousing, and distributing stock. The money for publishers, then, is generally in books that have long lives in backlist.

The paperback may have a new jacket and may involve a new push by the publisher. Paperbacks reach a different market—perhaps younger and generally wider, since many readers' budgets don't allow for frequent purchases of hardcovers. The new push also may reflect the successes and failures of publishing the hardcover. The publisher may have learned that your book has appeal for a different audience than originally anticipated. If there has been critical acclaim, the evidence of that will likely appear on the paperback in the form of endorsements on the cover.

In the meantime, you may be sick of the whole thing. You may wish you had written an entirely different book. You may forget what it is you wrote. You may have come to hate aardvarks. Never mind all that—be a pro and stand behind your work and your publisher, at least in public. And keep smiling.

Why? Because even if you are angry at your editor and sick of the subject matter, you want your publisher to succeed with your book. This is not because you are a saint, though you may be—it is because publishers keep winners, even modest ones, in print. If your books are still available, there is more opportunity for people to learn about your work and look for other books you've written. And then there are royalties. These probably won't be huge, but if your book stays in print long enough and "earns out"—that is, when the book has sold enough for the publisher to have made back 100 percent of the advance money paid to you—you will begin getting royalties. This never happens for the majority of books, so if it does for yours, be proud.

In the meantime you can help with this process. Continue to expand your platform (however silly that sounds) by speaking, writing, watching out for media opportunities, and developing your online presence. When you do go to speak somewhere, make sure your hosts have copies of your book ahead of time, and also keep a supply of your own books on hand, as you may need to bring and even sell your own books on occasion. Maintain and increase your e-mail list and contacts.

Another important thing you can do is start writing a new book. It's possible, even likely, that the new book will be related in some way to the first book. But whatever you choose to write, this gives you a positive outlet for your energies. So go for it. That's what authors do—write. Plus, it will give you something to talk about when people ask you what you are working on now.

ROYALTIES AND OTHER POST-PUBLICATION BIZ

The typical royalty statement is a mystifying document—don't feel bad if you don't understand yours. You can ask your agent or editor to explain it to you, as each publisher's format is slightly different. Royalties are computed via a mathematical system devised by Martians, but the basic idea is that the publisher pays you an advance and then waits until that advance is recouped (and returns are computed, a process that can apparently take years) in book sales before forking over any additional payments. Once your advance is recouped, royalties reflect "sell through"—or how many copies of your book have actually sold to customers. This is not the same as how many were ordered by stores. You can expect an obtuse and mystifying royalty statement twice a year.

GLOSSARY OF PUBLISHING TERMINOLOGY

Make these commonly used publishing terms part of your vocabulary and you'll sound like a pro.

A

Acetate
A transparent plastic sheet with images, sometimes in layers showing different printing elements such as an embossed title, or placed over artwork to protect it and to allow the designer to write instructions

Acid-free paper
Paper that resists yellowing from age, made with pulp processed with little or no acid

Acknowledgments
Preliminary pages in which the author thanks the people who helped create the book or provided other kinds of support, and a good place for aspiring authors to research the names of agents; believe it or not, this isn't the most important part of your book—try to avoid thanking "everyone who made this possible" (e.g., your second-grade teacher, the guy who sold you all those lattes, your cat)

Advance
Money paid to the writer before publication; this amount is offset against the royalties the book will earn—don't spend it all in one place

Advance copies
Books the publisher or printer sends to reviewers, media, and other interested parties before the publication date

Agent, agency (also literary agent or agency)
A person or organization representing authors, selling their work for publication, negotiating contracts; there are many versions of a classic joke about agents, but we won't tell them here because the Author Enablers is a family friendly operation, but the punch line

is always, "My agent came to my *house?!*" (Because, well, that isn't going to happen.)

Artwork
Photographs and illustrations

Author questionnaire
A document the author fills out to identify marketing and publicity opportunities for the publisher

Author's copies
Complimentary copies given to an author on publication; you never get enough, so avoid the temptation to give them to everyone you listed in your acknowledgments

Author's corrections (AC)
Author's corrections at proofing stage

B

Backlist
Older books in the publisher's catalogue that are not necessarily being actively promoted but are still in print and available

Bar code
The ugly machine-readable code printed on products, used for pricing and tracking inventory

Big-mouth list
A list of prominent figures who can help get the word out about your book. Often publishers send these people a galley or finished book

Binding
To join pages or signatures (set amount of pages derived from one larger sheet of paper) with stitching, glue, etc.

Bleed
Layout that extends beyond the trim marks on a page; printed images bleed if they go to the edge of the page; also, what your fingers do if you spend too much time at the keyboard; also, what your heart does every time your manuscript gets rejected

Blind folio
An unprinted page

Block (aka book block)
Bound pages of a book before the cover is added

Blockhead
The editor who rejected your manuscript

Blog
An op-ed or journal-style; there are 7 trillion blogs on the planet with an average readership of 0.2 people, but you need to do one anyway; make yours better

Blueline
Marks with special pencil on proof that do not show up on printing plates

Blurb
A short endorsement of a book and/or the author, used in publicity efforts and often printed on the jacket or a teaser page

Body or body text
The main text of the book, not including the headlines, front and back matter, etc.

Boilerplate
Repetitive type; template

Bonuses (aka escalators)
Additional money paid to the author based on the work meeting certain goals (for example a certain amount paid for every week a book makes the *New York Times* bestseller list) set out in the writer's contract

Bound galleys or advance reading copies (ARCs) or advance reader's editions (AREs)
Uncorrected page proofs that are bound like a paperback and sent to review outlets to generate pre-publication publicity or to get endorsements (often called "blurbs")

Bullet
A large dot preceding text that sets that text off from the running text

Buzz
The excitement generated by word-of-mouth interest, rapidly spread

C

Calligraphy
Fine or ornamental handwritten text

Caption
Text identifying a picture or illustration

Coated paper
Paper that is chemically treated for a smoother finish

Co-publishing
The simultaneous publishing of a work by more than one publisher, usually for different markets

Copyright
Legal protection granted to the originator of material to prevent use without permission

Copyright page
The page at the beginning of a book with copyright and Library of Congress information

Course adoption
Utilization of a book as a required text in academic classes

Crop marks
Printed lines showing where to trim a printed sheet

D

Deckle edge
A rough edge left on some paper; not to be confused with a low-cut blouse

Dedication
A tribute in the front of the book from the author to a person, persons, or cause; what it takes to finish your book

Desk copy
A copy requested by an educational institution interested in adopting the title for a course

Dingbat
An ornamental element that denotes a space break in the text; everyone who turns down your book

Dots-per-inch (DPI)
A measure of resolution in printing. It refers to dots of ink used by a printing device. In general, the more dots (higher DPI) used, the clearer the image

Drop cap
A large initial letter at the start of the text that drops into the line or lines of text below

Dummy
A mockup of the book layout at finished size; everyone who turns down your book

E

Earning out
The point when enough copies of the book have sold to cover the amount of the publisher's advance

E-book
A book in digital form

E-book reader
The portable electronic device with which one reads an e-book

Embargo
A process whereby the sale of a book is restricted, by publisher's edict, until an agreed-upon moment in time (think *Harry Potter*)

Embossing
The process of creating a three-dimensional image or design in the paper or cover

End papers
The pages at the front and back of a book pasted to the cover boards

F

Foil embossing or stamping
The process of stamping a design on a book cover without ink, using a colored foil with pressure from a heated die or block

Foldout or gatefold
An oversized sheet bound into a publication, frequently used for a map or chart; not to be confused with a centerfold

Font
A specific size and style of type within a type family or typeface

Foreword
Introductory text in the front matter that is written by someone other than the author, often an authority on the subject of the book

Four-color process
Printing in full color using four color separation negatives (yellow, magenta, cyan, and black)

French flaps
Extensions of the cover of a paperback that fold back inside the book and contain extra copy, imitating the flaps of the jacket of a hardcover book

Frontlist
The publisher's newest books; for accounting purposes, the books published in a fiscal year; for sales, generally books during their first year after publication

Front matter
Everything before the first chapter or beginning of the main text of the book

G

Galley (or bound galley)
Pre-publication copies of a book to be sent out for reviews and endorsements (but not for sale); the kitchen on a boat

Galley proof
Copy of text for checking by the author and publisher before the manuscript is assembled for the print run

Ghostwriter
Someone who is paid to write a book for which authorship will be credited to another; Charles Dickens

Gilding
Gold leaf on the edge of the pages; what you shouldn't do to the lily

Gloss
A shiny look that is achieved with ink that dries without penetration

Gutter
The inside margins toward the book's bound edge; where Edgar Allen Poe met his end

H

Half-title page
A page that includes only the title of the book

House style
Copyediting rules in a publishing house for punctuation, capitalization, etc.

I

Imprint
The publisher; larger publishers often have a number of different imprints, each with a different focus

Introduction
Material at the beginning of the main text that explains or presents the book to the reader; the introduction is always by the author

ISBN
Acronym for International Standard Book Number, used as the title's digital identity for inventory, tracking sales, and pricing (see bar code)

K

Kerning
Adjustment of spacing between certain letter pairs

Kill fee
Prenegotiated fee paid to a writer by a publisher when a contracted book is not published

L

Landscape
Print format or layout in which the width is greater than the height

Leaf
A sheet of paper

List
All the books that a publisher has in print or that are forthcoming; often divided into sections identified by season or chronology (e.g. spring list, fall list, backlist, frontlist)

Long discount
The discount generally given by trade publishers to booksellers of 40 to 50 percent off a book's list price; academic books usually come with a 20 percent, or short, discount

M

Manuscript (ms)
The original work by the author

Margins
Nonprinted areas of the page

Mark up copy
Copy prepared with typesetting instructions

Mass-market books
Inexpensive paperback editions, often sold in airports, supermarkets, and mega-stores, the successful authors of which never win the National Book Award but make boatloads of money

Matte finish
Nonglossy paper or ink finish

Mechanical
Camera-ready art

Mechanical separation
A method utilizing plastic sheet overlays for each color used in the printing process; when you have a fight with the person who fixes your car

Midlist
Books that are not lead titles or bestsellers but that have a shot at doing well enough to justify being published—the majority of books fall into this category

Mock-up
The rough visual model for a book design

N

Newsprint
Low-quality paper like that used for newspapers

O

One-day lay-down
Applies to major titles (think *Harry Potter*) that are released for sale at one agreed-upon moment in time, e.g., midnight on Halloween; the 24-hour flu

On-sale date
The agreed-upon date when a book can be sold by all retailers

Option clause
Contractual clause that gives the publisher the right of first refusal on an author's next book

Orphan
1. instance of the first line of a paragraph sitting by itself at the bottom of a page; 2. a book or author whose editor leaves the company

during the publication process; 3. character in a Charles Dickens novel

Out of print
Status of a book when it is no longer offered for sale by the publisher, often accomplished informally by letting the title go out of stock

Over the transom
Unsolicited manuscripts that are submitted without agent representation

P

Page count
Total number of pages including blank pages

Page proof (or first pass)
Stage following galley proofs where type and sometimes graphics are laid out as they will look in the printed book

PDF (Portable Document Format)
Widely used format for Adobe Acrobat Reader that makes it possible to send formatted documents and have them appear, exactly as designed, on the recipient's monitor or printer

Perfect bind
Sheets and cover bound with glue, common for paperback books; a tricky situation that drives the plot of your thriller

Permissions
The requirement that any proprietary work (song lyrics, poetry, artwork) have permission cleared by the owner of the rights, often involving payment of a fee

Platform
The audience, contacts, organization, and fame of the author

Portrait
An upright image or page where the height is greater than the width

Pre-emptive offer
A publisher's bid that prevents a project from going to auction

Preface
Text at the front of a book that explains or introduces it to the reader. This is the author's own statement, and may include acknowledgments. It follows the foreword, if there is one, and is part of the front matter.

Proof
An initial typeset and designed version of the book or the cover, produced to correct errors and make alterations

Proof correction marks
Standard set of signs and symbols in the margin to indicate corrections on proofs

Publication (or pub) date
A date set by the publisher before which news media are not supposed to review the book; this is to allow time for transportation from the warehouse to booksellers, and may be from four to eight weeks after the finished book is available

R

Reading line
A descriptive line of text that appears on the book jacket or cover but isn't the official subtitle

Recto
The right-hand page of an open book; the standard side to start a story or chapter

Release date
The day on which a book is scheduled to be shipped to bookstores and/or is ready for sale; this comes before both the on sale and publication dates

Remainder
The fate of books that are printed in much too large a quantity for subsequent sales; the resulting discounts at extremely low prices are beneficial to the consumer, but not the author or publisher

Review copy
Book copy sent to the media in the hope that they will publish a review or promote the book

Rock Bottom Remainders
A mediocre rock band made up of famous authors and "rock stars in residence," with the stated purpose of raising money for literacy-related charities; the band's members include (or have included) Stephen King, Dave Barry, Amy Tan, Scott Turow, Mitch Albom, Tad Bartimus, Dave Marsh, Greil Marcus, Joel Selvin, Ridley Pearson, James McBride, Roy Blount Jr., Matt Groening, Barbara Kingsolver, Robert Fulghum, Roger McGuinn, Warren Zevon, Al

Kooper, and—by astonishing coincidence—Sam Barry and Kathi Kamen Goldmark (She founded the band in 1992)

Running head or footer
Line of type at the top of a page which repeats the heading or other information on each page; the Headless Horseman in Washington Irving's alternate universe

Running text
This is a fancy term for the way most people write—forming words into sentences, which are in turn formed into paragraphs. In other words, your basic prose

S

Saddle stitch
To bind by stapling sheets together in the seam where the sheets fold; how a cowboy mends his trousers

Sample chapter
A sample of the manuscript included in a book proposal

Sell through
The percentage of books shipped that are actually sold by retailers (a 50 percent or higher sell through is considered respectable); in current practice, most unsold titles are returned to the publisher

Short discount
The discount generally given by trade publishers on academic books of 20 percent off a book's list price; trade books usually come with a 40 to 50 percent, or long, discount

Slush pile
The unsolicited (over-the-transom) manuscripts that lie around on editorial assistants' desks or languish in e-mail inboxes; the sidewalk outside Random House in early March

Spine
Back or binding edge of a book or publication

Spiral bind
Continuous wire or plastic looped through holes along bound edge

Stet
Proof correction that rescinds a correction (The copyeditor of our book says "Oh no! We don't like authors to know they can stet" but she doesn't mean *you.*)

Stock
Paper for printing

Style sheet
A list of words, terms, and phrases that a copyeditor maintains for a manuscript so that the book will be consistent (e.g., do or don't capitalize "church")

T

Table of contents (TOC)
Listing of the divisions of the book (e.g., chapters) and the pages on which they begin

Teaser page

A page or pages at the beginning of the book that promotes the book by offering praise for the author's writing, a sample of the contents, or some other promotional material

Template

Layout with basic page dimensions; the thing you serve "tem" on

Thumbnail

A small version of an image or, if plural, small versions of images

Tip in

The insertion of an extra page in a book after the normal printing process is completed

Title page

A page that includes the title, author's name, and possibly other information such as the translator or publisher

Track

Sales record of an author's previous books

Trade publisher

A company that publishes for the general consumer market

Trim size

The book's finished size

Typo

Typographical errur

U

UV coating
Laminated paper treated with ultraviolet light

V

Varnish
Clear liquid applied after printing for glossy appearance and protection

Vellum
A thick, rough book paper (originally an ancient form of paper made from the treated skin of a calf)

Verso
The left-hand page of a book

W

Widow
Instance of the last line of a paragraph left alone at the top of a page

INDEX